MEGALITHIC TOMBS
AND OTHER
ANCIENT REMAINS
IN THE DECCAN

MEGALITHIC TOMBS
AND OTHER
ANCIENT REMAINS
IN THE DECCAN

MEADOWS TAYLOR

GYAN

Published by

GYAN

Gyan Publishing House
5, Ansari Road
Daryaganj, New Delhi-110002
Phone: 011-47034999, 9811692060
E-mail: books@gyanbooks.com

Distribution Network
gyanbooks.com
India, USA, Canada, UK, Australia, France

ISBN : 978-81-212-3769-7 (PB)
First Published, 1941

2nd Impression 2020

Printed at: Gyan Press, Delhi.

Megalithic Tombs and Other Ancient Remains In the Deccan
Author: Meadows Taylor

PREFACE

MEADOWS TAYLOR is still a name to conjure with in the State of Hyderabad. The romantic events of his life are most vividly recorded in his autobiography, *The Story of my Life*, but he also possessed a scientific frame of mind, and was a keen observer of the geographical and geological features of the country through which he happened to pass, and an ardent student of the habits, beliefs and history of the people among whom he lived. His *History of India* amply corroborates this view, but to an archæologist the most interesting and valuable among his works are his papers on the megalithic remains of the Deccan which he has described in great detail. They show his scientific knowledge and wide study of the subject. Two of these papers, *The Ancient Remains at the Village of Jivarji*, and *Notices of Cromlechs, Cairns and other Ancient Scytho-Druidical Remains in the Principality of Sorapur*, were published in the Journal of the Bombay Branch of the Royal Asiatic Society, Vols. III and IV for 1851 and 1852 respectively, and another which is profusely illustrated and bears the title, *Description of Cairns, Cromlechs, Kistvaens and other Celtic, Druidical or Scythian Monuments in the Deccan*, was printed in the Transactions of the Royal Irish Academy (Vol. XXIV, Part III., pp. 329-62) in May 1862. As these Journals are not easily available in India, and the information contained in them is of immense value for all those who want to make a survey or detailed study of the megalithic tombs of the Deccan, I approached my friend, Mr. C. E. A. W. Oldham, C.S.I., Secretary of the Royal Asiatic Society of Great Britain and Ireland, with the request that he would kindly have copies of these articles made for me, so that they may be reprinted for the use of present-day student. Mr. C. E. A. W. Oldham readily complied with my request and arranged for the copying of the letterpress as well as the illustrations of these three articles through Miss L. M. Anstey of the India Office, and I take this opportunity to thank both of them for their kind help in this connection.

In order to keep the memory of Meadows Taylor always fresh in the minds of the people of the Deccan, Sir Theodore Tasker, C.I.E., O.B.E., I.C.S., the Revenue Member of H.E.H. the Nizam's

Government, had proposed that the house of Meadows Taylor at Shorapur should be preserved and some of the rooms of the building used as a commemorative Museum, equipped with articles which either belonged to Meadows Taylor, or are referred to in his studies. The Rt. Hon'ble Sir Akbar Hydari, P.C., D.C.L., who by nature has a reverential regard for all those who have added to human knowledge and culture, readily sanctioned the scheme and it is hoped that the Meadows Taylor's Memorial Museum, located in his own house, will soon become an accomplished fact. It is proposed to keep in the Museum a complete set of his works for study and some of them will also be on sale. The reprinting of these three papers has been done mainly with the latter object.

G. YAZDANI

Hyderabad-Deccan
2nd February, 1941.

Reprinted from the Journal of the Bombay Branch of the Royal Asiatic Society for January 1851, Vol. III (pp. 179-193)

ARTICLE II

ANCIENT REMAINS AT THE VILLAGE OF JIWARJI NEAR FEROZABAD ON THE BHIMA

By Captain Meadows Taylor

The ancient remains at the village of Jiwarji though somewhat different in character from those at Rajan Kaloor and Hegaratgi (Hajinitji), are yet identical in many respects with them, and whether more or less ancient, appear evidently to belong to the same family as the Celtic and Druidical or Scythic remains of England and Brittany, where they abound, as well as in Denmark, Russia and Circassia, and in parts of India, where those of the Nilgherries and the hill country to the southward of them are perhaps the most remarkable and abundant.

My own speculations on the identity of the "Cromlechs," and "Kistvaens," of Rajan Kaloor and Hegaratgi, with the Druidical remains of Anglesea and the other parts of Great Britain, led me to assume that they belonged to the same religion and people, however widely apart as to situation ; and my speculations, dim and undefined as they were, have been lately confirmed in a great measure by the perusal of a very interesting paper on the subject of the monumental remains of the Nilgherries by Captain H. Congreve, Madras Army, which was published in No. XXXII, January to June 1847, of the *Madras Journal of Literature and Science,* and which as far as my opinion goes, entirely justifies the assumption that the remains on the Nilgherries were those of Indo-Scythian tribes whose faith was Druidical, and who, nomadic in their habits, entered India at an early period, eventually settled there, and have their representatives in the modern Todawars or Thautawars of the Nilgherries, a race which still preserves the dress and food, mode of sacrifice and sepulture, and many of the customs of their progenitors and have avoided idolatry.

To attempt any analysis of Captain Congreve's valuable and interesting paper would be impossible here, nor is it needed further than as authority in reference to what has come under my own observation; but all things considered, whether in relation to the size and perfect condition of the remains at Jiwarji, their great number, and absolute identity of form and contents with others referred to, I am induced to suppose that there are no more remarkable collections in India, if perhaps in the world, except those at Yemmi Good near Kanagerry which were described to me by a native as greater in extent, larger, and more ornamented than the Cromlechs of Rajan Kaloor.* I now regret that I had not the whole of the Cromlechs and Kistvaens at Rajan Kaloor and Hegaratgi counted, but I may be able to make another visit to the place this year, when this essential particular will not be omitted. It is evident that the remains at Yemmi Good would be well worth a visit.

The Scythic Druidical remains whether of England or Brittany, etc., have three general characteristics, viz., Cromlechs, Kistvaens and Cairns, Barrows, etc., the latter of various forms.

First Cromlechs, or stone Moles, are constructed with three flat stones or slates placed edgeways in the ground enclosing three sides of a square or parallelogram, as supports or walls, with one at the top as a cover usually larger than the others, and having one side open, usually the north or north-west. There is usually also a flooring of slabs. These Cromlechs

* Does it refer to the Benkal group of 'dolmens' which is the finest and the most extensive in the Dominions? The Benkal 'dolmens' are not far from Kanakgiri.—*G.Y.*

re not as numerous at Rajan Kaloor and Hegaratgi as the Kistvaens or closed Cromlechs, but there are still many, and all exactly correspond with the Cromlech called Kitts Coty House near Aylesford in Kent, (a small one),. with those at Plas Newydd in Anglesea, and those in Brittany and the Nilgherries. The most remarkable of the remains as to size, in England, is one of those at Plas Newydd, the dimensions of which are given as follows : viz., upper slab 12 feet 7 inches long by 12 feet broad and 4 feet thick, supported bv five stones forming the sides of the enclosure.

On reference to the drawing and measurements of one at Rajan Kaloor, I observe that they are as follows: viz., upper slab or cover 12 feet 3 inches long by 10 feet 6 inches broad, side slabs 12 feet long by 7 feet high, including 2 feet in the ground, there were others differing very little indeed in measurement, and all forming noble groups. The style of erection is precisely the same in every respect with the European and Nilgherry ones, and the dimensions of the interiors also closely correspond with them.

Annexed are tracings (Plate I, Figs. 1, 2) from the drawings of Cromlechs given by Captain Congreve. I did not find funeral remains such as urns or other earthen vessels in any Cromlech opened, and this tallies with results elsewhere observed. The Cromlechs therefore have been Altars, as supposed in England, or covered Temples in which funeral ceremonies were performed. Several of the Cromlechs at Rajan Kaloor, are surrounded by a circle of stones. This corresponds with the Cromlechs at Trer Dryn in Anglesea, and other places referred to by Captain Congreve, as also on the Nilgherries.

Second Kistvaens or closed Cromlechs. These are described as existing in England and Wales, "frequently occurring in those places most favoured by the Druids." They form the majority of the monuments at Rajan Kaloor and Hegaratgi, and appear of precisely the same construction as those in England, and on the Nilgherry hills. Captain Congreve mentions them as occurring on the Mailgherry hills, 30 miles south of Ooxoor, at Naikenary on the top of the pass of that name, also in Malabar, Ungadapoor and Mungary, in south Coimbatore, in Travancore, and one at Pulliconda near Vellore.

Captain Kittoe, quoted by Captain Congreve, finds them in the forests of Orissa,—" at this place Goorsunk, I remarked a number of stones placed in the same manner as the Druidical monuments, such as Kitts Coty House near Boxley in Kent ; viz., three (stones) set upright with one on the top of them. These houses are very small, etc."

Those at the Nilgherries and those I have found, are the same in one very remarkable particular, viz., the circular aperture in one stone or monolith, as if left, as Captain Congreve suggests, for the introduction of urns from time to time. Their size differs greatly from the smallest square of 18 inches to 2 feet, to the largest of 6 to 7 feet long and 5 feet broad. Only the largest have circular apertures. In the smaller ones, the top slab or cone might be removed and replaced without much inconvenience. Captain Congreve thus describes some near the fort of Adi Raer Cottay on the Nilgherries :—

> " In the sequel I ascertained that about a mile beyond Adi Raer Cottay there were some stone edifices ascribed by the Burghas to the former Dwarf inhabitants of the Hills."
>
> " The Kistvaens were nearly buried in the vegetable soil, a fact considering their height (five feet), that sufficiently attests the high antiquity that may be assigned to them. When these structures occur in the low country they are found on the summits or sides of rocky hills

devoid of jungle, and hence appear in the state they were originally constructed, unencumbered with soil or rubbish. After removing a large slab five feet long, three broad and one thick, which served as the roof of one of the closed Cromlechs, I proceeded to excavate the earth that had fallen inside, and reached the floor, another large flag eight feet long by six broad; here I found fragments of clay vessels, probably remains of funeral urns. The chamber being cleared, presented four walls, each consisting of an entire stone, and was seven feet long by five broad. The monolith constituting the eastern wall was pierced by a circular aperture about nine inches in diameter, adequate to admit the body of a child who I conjecture was employed to place the urns inside."

The belief is prevalent at Jiwarji, that the "Mora" people, supposed dwarfs of three spans high, constructed the remains at Rajan Kaloor, Yemmi Good, Hegaratgi, etc. These remains are also attributed to fairies and dwarfs by the superstitions of Wales, Dorsetshire, Cornwall, Brittany, etc.

The monuments at Rajan Kaloor and Hegaratgi are on bare open spots, and gentle rises from rivulets. The ground is hard rock or strong morum a foot to 8 inches from the surface, and the Cairns and Barrows at Jiwarji, are also on a hard gravelly elevation which has only a thin surface soil.

The whole of Captain Congreve's description exactly tallies with what I saw at Rajan Kaloor and Hegaratgi, and the circular aperture in the monolith or slab of the side marks the identity very strikingly. Captain Congreve states the aperture to have been in the east side or wall, but in those I examined, it was uniformly, I think, in the south side or south-west. No other remains appear to have been found in the Kistvaens either of England or the Nilgherries, but urns with ashes and bones, mixed with charcoal, which tallies precisely with my own experience.

Images were found in some of the Cairns, etc., in the Nilgherries. I have found none at Jiwarji yet, nor have any that I am aware been found in Brittany or England. This would appear to class those in England, these at Jiwarji, and those in the Nilgherries in which no images were found, (the Kistvaens for instance) as the earliest, and those in the Nilgherries in which images were found, as belonging to a later class; probably corrupted by Buddhism or Jainism, which was powerfully established in the hills and in the plains below them, throughout Mysore. Druidism was not idolatry, but degenerated into it, perhaps through the Scandinavians or other Celto-Scythic tribes, and so passed into England. There is a strong affinity between Woden and Buddh or Bodh, and by many they are supposed to be the same. Could then idolatry have begun in India from Buddhism, and have spread westwards through the Druidical religion so corrupted by the Buddhists?

It may be presumed, I think, that the absence of images in Kistvaens and Cromlechs justifies an assumption for them of a higher antiquity and purer Druidical faith than the Cairns, Barrows, etc., in which images are found.

We see therefore that the circular aperture in one monolith is common to the Kistvaens of Europe, of the Nilgherries (Congreve), of Circassia (Bell), and of Rajan Kaloor, etc. The size, construction, situation in groups, contents as to ashes mixed with charcoal, etc., etc., all agree in the minutest particulars. Subjoined are tracings (Figs. 3, 4: Pl. I) from the drawings of a Kistvaen given by Captain Congreve. There were scores of the size given by Captain Congreve, both at Rajan Kaloor and Hegaratgi, as well as smaller ones, down to the sizes like three-legged stools, noted by Captain Kittoe.

Third Cairns and Barrows. These are found sparingly with the Kistvaens and Cromlechs in comparison with themselves.

They consist of circles of large stones, sometimes single, sometimes double, enclosing a space under which is a grave, or graves, a stone-chest, or chests, in which bodies and sometimes funeral urns have been deposited. I need hardly say that, with the Cromlechs, they are common to England, France, Germany, Central Asia and parts of India, and though minor details of form and of the articles found in them differ in unimportant respects, the general results are everywhere the same, and the form and mode of sepulture identical.

They appear to be divided into two classes, one which contains urns, etc., having been filled with human ashes, bones and *charcoal,* and the other in which bodies have been interred *without* urns, filled with ashes or *charcoal*, but accompanied by rude images, arms, earthen, iron and brass utensils and the like. These may be of an era subsequent to the first, and when, though the old custom of sepulture had not been abandoned, the rude but simple faith of older times had been corrupted by idolatry.

Be this as it may, Captain Congreve's patient investigations on the Nilgherries, shew a variety of results in regard to the forms of the Cairns or Barrows, minor points differing even there, also in the nature of the relics found, but none in regard to the general features, mode of sepulture, etc., between his results and those of parties in England by whom similar remains have been explored. The same kind of vases or urns containing ashes mixed with charcoal, the urns being of good strong pottery with a peculiar glaze of a rich *red* colour, knives, spearheads, etc., are found in Dorsetshire as on the Nilgherries. Brass cups, beads, and often a bell, are common to both the latter, forming the strongest presumptive link that the Thautawars, to whom a bell in the sacred Dairy is an object of worship still, are the remains of these Scytho-Druidical tribes in India.

At Rajan Kaloor there are many Cairns and Barrows interspersed with the Cromlechs and Kistvaens, some of these have small Kistvaens in the centre, some open at top, others closed, others have no Kistvaens but a stone only to mark the centre, but all or most have two slabs of stones set on edge about 2 feet asunder, forming as it were, an entrance to the grave on the south or south-west side, a peculiarity which I do not find mentioned by Captain Congreve, or alluded to by him as existing in England.

The foregoing will give a general idea of the connection almost identical, between the three general classes of European Scytho-Druidical remains, and those of the Nilgherries, Rajan Kaloor and Hegaratgi, and I have no doubt whatever, that the Cromlechs and Kistvaens, etc., of Yemmi Good near Kanagerry would, if examined, contribute their full share to the elucidation of this most interesting subject of investigation.

I proceed now to describe the remains at Jiwarji. This village, one of the Kusbas of the Andola Taluk, is situated about three miles south of the Bhima river on the high road between Calburgah, Ferozabad and Shorapur. About a mile from it, immediately to the right of the high road to Ferozabad, upon a rising ground sloping to the south, there are a great number of Cairns and Barrows, filling the area of a parallelogram of 336 by 216 yards. Having had the whole carefully counted, I found there were, small and large, 375. These Cairns and Barrows are of all sizes, varying from diameters of 40 feet inside the circle of stones to 68 and 10 feet respectively; some of them have single circles, others double, the double ones being usually the largest Cairns, though not always. The number of stones in these circles varies from 24 to 36 in the single circles, and from 48 to 58 in the double ones. Where the circles are double, they are from 3 to 4 feet apart, the stones forming them, being placed touching each other or at short intervals. I observed that in some Cairns with double circles, the space between the circles had been neatly paved with small flat slabs of slaty limestone, portions of which remain. Some of the Cairns have small square enclosures in the centre, probably Kistvaens, from which the top may have been removed; these are always composed of four slabs of limestone set upright, which project about a foot, more or less above the surface. The space enclosed being from 2 to 3 feet square. The circles of the large Barrows or Cairns are composed of large trap boulders which have evidently been brought from the rising ground to the westward about a mile distant, where the trap meets the limestone formation. These black circles of stones therefore make the Cairns very remarkable objects, as the soil they are upon is a very light coloured limestone, and as there is little or no vegetation the stones have not been covered by grass or earth, or very slightly. I should mention also that some of the Cairns have long stone-chests formed of thin slabs of limestone laid edgeways, upright, and projecting a little above the surface. None of these have tops or lids, and the graves (as these were), no doubt have been filled in, (as well as the spaces enclosed by the circles of stones), with loose stones and earth, the hard ground below not having been dug into. Possibly these were graves of the poorer members of the tribe who could not afford deep excavations.

In all, however large, the space within the circle-stones, has been filled up with loose stones and earth, rising towards the centre. The entrance-stones as I may perhaps call them are from 5 to 6 feet long, and 4 to 5 feet high, and have been let into the earth or stones from 3 to 4 feet. Fig. 5 (Pl. I) is a profile of one of these Cairns and corresponds exactly with one of the drawings of some Cairns in Captain Congreve's paper. I am thus particular in description as it may be interesting and important to observe the similarity or difference which exists between these and Cairns at other places.

Having selected one of the largest and most perfect for excavation (Plate II, Fig. 6), I found it of the following dimensions. Diameter of the inside circle 40 feet, outside circle 48 feet, space between the stone-circles, including the stones, 4 to 6 feet. Two upright slabs of limestone about 5 feet long and 2 feet asunder, appeared about 18 inches above the surface of the Cairns, and near them on the south-west side I began the excavation. These slabs lay north-east and south-west, or nearly so, and the same may be remarked of all similar stones and Kistvaens in this Cemetery. A space of 10 feet wide was marked off in the direction of the stones across the Cairns, and the surface-excavation was confined to this breadth, as I considered that such a trench would completely expose the contents of the Cairns whatever they might be. The loose stones and earth continued to a depth of 4 feet 8 inches in the centre, in a circle of 8 feet diameter, the sides gradually sloping upwards to the surface circle-stones. Below the loose stones, the ground was very hard and firm, scarcely yielding to the pickaxe, being morum which had formed into a concrete mass. But as nothing had appeared among the loose stones, either urns or stone-chest, I determined to dig as deeply as possible, supposing that so considerable a Cairn could not be without remains, and I directed the centre to be explored to the depth of at least 6 feet more.

The strong earth and morum continued for 4 feet, when a corner slab of limestone appeared, laid transversely, which having been removed, the workmen found a few bits of broken pottery and an earthen saucer that broke on the touch. The earth having been further cleared away, other transverse pieces of stone were found and afterwards the sides of two upright slabs of limestone appeared, across which the transverse pieces had been laid as it were to form a lid, there was no longer doubt therefore that this was the coffin or stone-chest, and the examination was carefully continued. The earth was however so hard and dry, that there appeared little hope of extricating any of the remains of pottery which now appeared, and the cross lid pieces of the stone-chest having broken from the superincumbent weight and fallen in, the earth above and beneath had become one mass.

The sides of the chest clearly appeared after a short time and then some portions of human leg-bones. On advancing further towards the head, the bones of the skeleton were more perfect, but so brittle that they could not be separated from the earth; at last a skull appeared, which after some contrivance came away whole. The body it belonged to, had been laid face downwards, and the impression of the face of the skull was perfectly distinct in the earth below. Fig. 7 is an outline of the upper part of the skull as far as the eye, taken from actual measurement. I had no drawing instruments with me and when I returned the next morning, I found to my regret that though the skull had been carefully put aside in a basket, the whole of the lower-jaw teeth, facial bones and nose had crumbled away. The profile of the face was peculiar, the chin having considerable projection, and the nasal bones being of unusual thickness and breadth. The two front teeth of the upper jaw were remarkably large and projected over the lower. The skull however appeared very small, but from the character of the teeth which were all perfect but one double one (which had been curious) and the firmness of the skull and its sutures, it was evidently that of a full-grown person. Below this body were two others, or their remains, but not so perfect as the upper one. The skull of one was remarkably thick and the head appeared to have been large. The length of two of the skeletons from the head to where the small bones of the toes were, were severally, the first 5 feet 7 inches, the second 5 feet 5½ inches, the third being undistinguishable. The bodies lay north-east and south-west, the heads being north-east. The only thing found in the chest was a single cornelian bead of an oblong cylindrical shape (Fig. 7, Plate I). Below the bodies, slabs of limestone had been placed to form a floor.

Immediately at the head of the bodies was a cross slab of limestone, and about 2 feet of the side slabs appearing to remain, the excavation was continued. Behind this cross-piece there seemed to have been placed one large earthen vessel and many small ones, with some earthen incense-burners. The large vessel was got out whole, the rest were entirely broken or fell to pieces on being exposed to the air. Continuing the excavation about 3 feet northward, the natural side of the tomb appeared, showing that the bounds of the grave had been reached. In this portion of the grave some pieces of iron, evidently spearheads, were found, but much decayed, and a weapon (Plate III) by them, but no ashes or charcoal, nor did the vessels contain anything but earth; probably it may have been the custom to fill the earthen pots with grain, milk, ghee, etc., and deposit them with the bodies at interment.

The earth appearing loose on each side of the stone-chest it was excavated down to the floor of the tomb. On the west side remains of two thin skeletons appeared of smaller size, possibly those of women, with some earthen incense-burners, etc., but the earth being soft and damp here they could not be removed. The eastern side was filled up with small earthen cups and vessels, incense-burners, etc., (Plate III), some of them were got out entire. They are very neatly made, and are either of red glazed pottery of a bright red colour or half red and half black. The glaze is inside as well as outside. By the side of these vessels, a small iron tripod and two spearheads much decayed were found. Some other pieces of iron were so decayed as to be undistinguishable in form.

The second Cairn examined had a double ring of stone measuring 16 feet in diameter, with 4 feet on each side, total 24 feet. The excavation was begun at the upright stones above the ground in the south-west side and a little below them were two large pieces of trap-rock. The loose stones continued to a depth of 3 feet, after which morum and earth to a depth of 5 feet 2 inches, making in all 8 feet. In the centre of the excavation the remains of a human body were found, but no portion of it was entire, portions of leg and thigh bones of great thickness and strength, and part of a very thick skull were all that was distinguishable. On the west and east sides of the body were the usual small earthen pots, etc., and in considerable quantity, but the concrete formed by the limestones, earth and morum was so hard that no entire vessel could be got out. With these were the remains of three spearheads of iron much decayed, but still distinguishable in form (Plate I).

There was no stone-chest or coffin in this Cairn and the body had been laid on the bare floor of the grave, which was 7 feet long by 4 broad, including the space taken up by the vessels on the east and west sides. The remnants of pottery were of the same colour and form as those of the first Cairn examined.

The third Cairn was 16 feet in surface diameter and had also a single ring of stones of large size, measuring usually 3 feet long, 2½ broad and 14 to 16 inches thick of irregular forms (trap boulders). It may be mentioned that the circle-stones of all the Cairns are the same size or thereabouts. The excavation was begun and carried down as in the others and continued to a depth of 8 feet 9 inches, of which the loose stones were 3 feet from the surface, and earth for the remainder. The earth in this Cairn was looser and more easily got out than in the others, and at the floor of the grave 14 small vessels of various sizes were obtained, some quite entire, others slightly cracked or chipped. No trace of former remains was found by them, but this may be attributable to the comparative soft quality of the earth, in which the body had doubtless entirely decayed. Some remnants of iron, and among them part of two heads of spears, and a flat pointed piece which may have been portion of a sword (Plate I). The earthen vessels were of the same colour, red and black, as those in the other Cairns, and all glazed.

The area at the bottom which contained these remains was 8 feet long by 7 wide. There was no stone-chest, nor upright slabs forming a lining for the sides or to contain the body.

The fourth Cairn had 24 feet of surface diameter and a double ring of stones, making in all 32 feet. The stones were of limestone breccia which is found near an adjacent rivulet. The same loose stones continued to a depth of 4 feet, after which there was gravelly earth. At a depth of 6 feet 6 inches from the top there were some transverse limestone slabs, of which a few were whole and others broken and fallen in; clearing away these carefully, the sides of two stone-chests or coffins appeared, that is, the two long slabs north and south, as nearly as possible, forming the outside boundaries of the chests, and one entire piece in the middle 1½ inches thick dividing the space into two, the whole length, was from 6 feet 6 inches to 7 feet, the breadth of each division 1 foot 8 inches. At the feet were upright slabs fitting closely into the breadth of each chest, and similar pieces 2 feet 8 inches high at a distance of 5 or 6 inches from the feet. The whole space enclosed therefore was 5 feet 6 inches long, 1 foot 10 inches high, and 1 foot 8 inches broad, the slabs being neatly put together.

The earth being carefully removed, the remains of one person in each grave were observed. The one to the east was more perfect than any yet seen, and the bones of the thighs and legs, pelvis, arms, etc., could be clearly traced though they broke on being touched. On removing the earth carefully from the head, it was found nearly whole resting upon its left side with the face to the earth. The teeth were entire in the upper jaw and their enamel still bright, and also enough of the skull to allow of my sketching the profile from actual measurement as it lay (Plate III, Fig. 14). The teeth of the upper jaw were large and remarkably thick, and projected somewhat over the lower ones. It was impossible to remove the skull entire as it had become decayed and adhered firmly to the stone-floor of the grave.

The entire length of this skeleton was 5 feet 2 inches from the crown of the skull to the feet, which had rested against the foot-slab, and there was a space of 4 inches between the skull and the upright head-stone of the chest. The skeleton to the west was not so long by 2 inches, but the bones of the legs and arms as also such portions of the skull as came away whole were much thicker and stronger.

The two head-slabs were next removed. Behind the eastern body were some remains of pottery and the legs of an iron tripod, one of which came away whole. The earth being further removed northward, a portion of a skull appeared which could not be got out entire. There were no other bones with it, and the head appeared to have been placed on the top of the earthen vessels with which the space was filled. Could this single skull have been the head of a person sacrificed at the funeral rites of the skeleton? I can give no other supposition than that it was; no such head appeared in any of the other tombs, and it may have been, from the evident care bestowed on the formation of this grave above the other small ones, that its occupants were persons of some consequence.

I did not attempt further excavations, as I considered that enough had been done to establish the identity of these remains with those of similar classes elsewhere. Whether this has been the case or not I leave those to decide who may be better judges in such matters than myself. But the following is a brief recapitulation of the principal points, not only as regards Cromlechs and Kistvaens, but as regards the Cairns at Jiwarji.

First the Cromlechs are exactly of the same construction with those of Europe and the Nilgherries, the sizes of the largest tallying with the principal ones which have been examined and measured elsewhere. They do not, as far as I have opened them, contain funeral remains, and therefore may have been Temples or Altars only for the performance of sacrifices or other ceremonies. The fact of their being associated with Kistvaens and Cairns in the same cemeteries, may give strength to this supposition. The traditions regarding those erected by dwarfs or fairies are identical with those of Europe, the Nilgherries, etc.

Second Kistvaens or closed Cromlechs. These also are identical with those of Great Britain and the Nilgherries, etc. They have all contained earthen urns, which have been filled with human ashes and bones mixed with charcoal, agreeing with the results obtained in England and in the Nilgherries. No idols or images have been found in any opened, nor have the urns had figures for handles or tops, but the colour of the earthen vessels is the same. The circular aperture in one of the monoliths of the Kistvaens, agrees entirely with that elsewhere noted, and is a remarkable feature in their identification.

Third Cairns and Barrows. These supply the same points of identification and resemblance with others. They are invariably round, and have either single or double circles of large stones or rocks round them. The centre is invariably elevated and consists of loose stones filled in over the earth of the grave below, to a depth of 3 to 4 feet. The graves contain stone-chests or coffins, or neat slabs of stone placed so as to form chests or coffins, covered by transverse slabs. These chests contain one or more bodies with earthen urns, etc., on three sides, east, north and west, none have been found to the south, or towards, the feet of the bodies. Portions of spearheads and other iron weapons have been discovered with the urns laid by the side of the bodies, but no images or idols as in some of the Nilgherry Cairns, nor any rings or brass vessels. The bodies are interred at a great depth from the surface varying from 8 to 10 feet.

Other particulars might perhaps be mentioned, but enough has been stated to prove I think the position I have assumed. The grand question now remains as to whose these monuments were. I have little doubt myself that they were those of nomadic tribes of Druidic Scythians who penetrated into India at a very early period and who must have formed local settlements in various parts, the last of which were probably in the Nilgherries. Some speculations have been made that these were the remains of Jains or Buddhists but we know the modes of sepulture in both castes to be entirely different from these, (and that arms were never buried with their dead) and had they been Hindu or Buddhist, it would have been impossible that they should not be much more numerous than they are. They are not sepultures of Hindus, who usually bury (where they bury), in a sitting posture, while those distinctive marks separate them from all other tribes except those who are acknowledged to be Druidical.

There has been I am aware much speculation on the subject of invasions of India by Scythic tribes from Central Asia, and the theories of Colonel Tod and others on the subject in regard to their amalgamation with Hindu tribes or identity with them must be familiar to all. We have however no trace of them subsequent to the invasions of Alexander. But Mr. Elphinstone quotes various authorities in regard to their invasions into India and partial occupation of the country in remote periods of antiquity. There can be little to affect the supposition or presumption that these people so far removed from their native land, may have become, as they settled, gradually mixed with the aborigines of the country and absorbed with them into the Hindu and Buddhist masses, and their funeral monuments are therefore interesting as showing how far they penetrated into India where they settled and how far they observed the rites and ceremonies of their ancient faith, in correspondence with the Druidical remains of Western Europe, and links which are found to obtain between—westwards and eastwards.

I have no knowledge of these remains in the central portion of India beyond those I have now described. I have heard that Cairns have been met with near Hyderabad, but am for the present entirely ignorant of their situation and number, and also whether they are accompanied by Cromlechs and Kistvaens or not. I myself have never observed any elsewhere, but that they may exist in greater numbers than these to the south and south-west may be inferred perhaps from the account of the remains at Yemmi Good, which may have been the great cemetery of the whole of this portion of India. Hindus collect the ashes of relations and carry them to the Ganges from all parts of India, and why not the Druidic Scythians to such places as were esteemed sacred by their tribes, which, from their nomadic character were, probably, widely scattered.

Reprinted from the Journal of the Bombay Branch of the Royal Asiatic Society for 1852, Vol. IV (pp. 380-429).

ART. IV.—NOTICES OF CROMLECHS, CAIRNS AND OTHER ANCIENT SCYTHO-DRUIDICAL REMAINS IN THE PRINCIPALITY OF SHORAPUR.

By

Captain Meadows Taylor.

Presented—October 1852.

IN a former communication I submitted to the Society some remarks upon the ancient Celtic-Scythian or Druidical Remains of the Shorapur District, and having understood from the Secretary that further details, accompanied, if possible, by plans of the various localities, would be acceptable, I have completed them as far as practicable, from time to time, and as I had opportunity during district tours, and now beg to transmit the result.

It has been very satisfactory to me to observe that the subject has excited considerable interest among antiquarians; and all the successive investigations I have made, have only the more strongly served to impress me with the belief, not only that the remains I have discovered here, and those that have been discovered by friends with whom I have been in communication in other parts of the country, are identical with those on the Nilgherris, but supply ample proof that they belong to the same race of Celtic-Scythian people, who, at a very early period in the history of man, penetrated westwards into Europe, and of whom such peculiar and striking memorials exist. I need not here recapitulate the grounds of this supposition—which are detailed in my former communication—further than to state, that as in Europe, the remains here are divided into three general classes :—

1st.—Cromlechs, or erections of large slabs of stones, generally open at one side, and formed of three large slabs for walls, and one for a roof. All the cromlechs I have seen are empty.

2nd.—Kistvaens, or erections smaller than the cromlechs, constructed on the same principle, but closed on all sides. In some of them a circular hole, from six to nine inches in diameter, exists in one of the sides ; and on removing one of the side-slabs, and opening out the interior, it is found to contain earthen pots, glazed with a red or black colour, which contain charcoal, earth, and portions of human bones and ashes— evidently the remains of the dead, which were collected after cremation, and finally deposited in these sepulchres. I may remark that these pots or urns are found covered with fine earth, which was probably placed over them as they were successively deposited. Whether it may be attributed to the greater age of the kistvaens over the cairns, or that more water or damp has found its way into them, I cannot say ; but though I have opened many kistvaens at Rājan-Kollur and Hegāratgi, I have not succeeded in obtaining any perfect urns from them, those that were found being so decayed and rotten that they could not be separated whole from the earth in which they were imbedded.

3rd.—Cairns, or small tumuli, surrounded with single, double, and treble circular rows of large stones or rocks ; of which, as regards contents, there were two varieties. In some, as at Jiwarji, Andola, etc., bodies have been buried, the skeletons of which are discoverable on excavation, accompanied by small and large urns, jars, fragments of iron weapons, tripods of iron, arrow and spear-heads, all the iron articles being very much decayed. Many of the smaller earthen vessels have been recovered in a perfect state from cairns which I have opened, and are well finished specimens of pottery, having a black or bright red glaze, or in some partially black and red inside and out. These cairns are by no means confined to the interment of one body : in some two, and in others remains of many adults and children could be traced by the pieces of skulls and bones ; while it was evident, also, that the children had been burned, and their bones and ashes interred in urns. In some cairns it was found that the bodies had been placed upon the natural floor of the grave, and the earth filled in ; but in the larger cairns there are cists or stone coffins, formed by slabs of limestone, with upright sides, and slabs as covers and for flooring, forming two and three coffins adjoining, in which were skeletons resting upon the ground-slabs or floor. Above the covering remains of other skeletons were found in some instances, particulars of which will be more fully noticed in their proper places. These cists or coffins were usually found at a depth of from twelve to fourteen feet from the surface, and it is evident that great care and labour was bestowed upon the construction of the graves. The other class of cairns, which do not differ in outward appearance from the others, contains large earthen pots or urns, of the same description of pottery, red and black, which are filled with charcoal and human ashes, and portions of bones and earth, evidently showing that after the burning of the dead the remains were collected and deposited in these cairns, as they were deposited in the kistvaens. From the above result it may be assumed that there were two sects of the same people, one of which burned their dead, and deposited the remains in kistvaens or cairns, and the other which buried their dead, and with them the weapons of the deceased, with probably funeral offerings of grain, etc., which were placed in the urns or jars, which in some instances nearly surround the stone cists in which the skeletons lie.

4th.—To these remains I am enabled from my investigations to add a fourth, which I have nowhere seen noticed before. There are large rocks, which have been placed regularly in diagonal lines, having open squares between each four rocks, the spaces in the squares being, most probably, and as will be explained more fully hereafter, intended for cairns. These remains are in many respects most curious and interesting : there might be doubts, perhaps, of their belonging to the same race, whose places of sepulture are so remarkable, if there were not cairns mingled with the rocks, showing, as will be seen by the plans, that they were placed as they exist by the same people.

The remains hitherto discovered by me exist in seven talooks or pergunnas of the Shorapur State—*Korikāl, Hunsgi, Malgatti, Rāstapūr, Maddarki, Andola,* and *Nellugi.* These adjoin each other, and reach from the SW. corner of the Shorapur territory in an irregular manner to the N. and NW., and from the Krishna river to the Bhima. It is evident that some spots were more favoured than others—whether as having been more sacred as burial-places, or whether as being near the location of large and permanent encampments, it is difficult to state. In the large cemeteries, as at Rājan-Kollur and Jiwarji, the remains cover a large space of ground, and are very numerous ; at the others, as will be seen by the plans, they are of smaller extent. In all situations, however, and whether in large or small groups, they perfectly preserve their several distinctive characters, I shall commence with the Korikāl talook, and take the others in order as they occur.

PLAN I.—CAIRNS AND KISTVAENS AT HEGĀRATGI.*

These are situated on a waste piece of land of a dry and gravelly character, about a mile and a half south of the village, near the bank of the Dône river : the ground slopes gently to the south, and is partially covered with low trees and bushes.

* See Plate V.

There is cultivation all round the spot adjoining, and among the cairns, many of which have been disturbed by the plough, but the kistvaens have been respected. There is no cromlech at this place. Of the twenty-three kistvaens, some are of large size, others much smaller. They are constructed of slabs of grey limestone, obtained from the eminences near, and these, in some instances, are of considerable size, and must have been transported with much difficulty and labour. Except in one instance, there is no difference in the arrangement of the erections here and at Rājan-Kollur: they are four large slabs of stone set upright in the earth, and covered by a fifth, which projects over the walls, forming effectual protection from the rains. One Kistvaen is, however, as remarkable for its size as for a peculiarity in the entrance, which I have not noticed elsewhere, and which may be thus illustrated :—

The front slabs form, as it were, an entrance enclosure in front of the sepulchre : the dimensions of the side slabs are very remarkable, being 15 feet 6 inches long, by 6½ feet high, and 4 inches thick. They are let into the ground about 2 feet, so that the erection was about 5 feet high in appearance. It had slabs laid down for a floor. This kistvaen was the most finished of any, and the most perfect. The sides appeared to fit closely, and there was no appearance of damp or decay ; but on examination it yielded nothing but the remains of pots or urns, none of which could be gotout entire, with portions of bones, ashes, and charcoal, mixed together. I much regretted afterwards that this fine specimen had been disturbed and broken in the examination, not having been present when it was opened. Two others were also examined, with the same result, but no cairns. It is evident, however, from their being in the same locality, that all belonged to the same tribe, and that it was of the sect which burned their dead, and buried their ashes. No remains of weapons, beads, arrow-heads, etc., were found in the kistvaens, and as the pots or urns which contained ashes and bones were for the most part much broken, it was almost impossible to discover how many had been deposited in each erection. In the largest there were distinct traces of seven large pots, with portions of others of smaller size, the number of which could not be ascertained. Some of the other larger kistvaens have sides measuring 13, 12, 10, and 9 feet respectively, by 4 to 7 feet broad or high, and the top-slabs in proportion. I did not measure the smaller ones, which are generally from 6 to 8 feet long, and 4 to 5 high.

PLAN II.—CROMLECHS AND KISTVAENS AT RĀJAN-KOLLUR.*

This very remarkable group of remains was the first which I had observed in this district; and though I had passed it on several occasions, each time with increased conviction that they could be no other than Celto-Druidic, from their exact resemblance to those in Wales, I forbore to come to any conclusion. On visiting them, however, in the latter end of 1850, in company with the late Dr. A. Walker, during a geological excursion, I halted at the village, and devoted some time to their examination. This convinced me that there was at least a curiously strong analogy, if no more, between these cromlechs and those of Wales, so strong that it amounted almost to conviction of their identity; and on Dr. Walker's return to Hyderabad he sent me the number of the *Madras Journal of Literature and Science* (No. xxxii) in which Captain Congreve's able article on the Druidical Remains on the Nilgherris is published. Perusal of this interesting narrative and detail left no doubt whatever on

* See Plate IV.

my mind in regard to my previous supposition. The style and plan of erection of these monuments—their size and contents—the peculiarity of the round hole in one of the end-slabs of some of the kistvaens—for it is not universal—the same traditional belief that they were the houses of fairies or dwarfs a span high, but endued with enormous strength, peculiar alike to Shorapur, the Nilgherris, Britain, France, etc., agreeing so minutely and perfectly in every locality—all combined to induce me to make the Society acquainted with the discovery of Druidic antiquities in the Dekhan which had not before been noticed, or suspected to exist.

The dimensions of these remains are very various, in fact of all sizes, from the largest cromlech, of which the south side is open, to the smallest possible enclosure, made by four slabs of stone, not exceeding in some instances 2 feet square, if so much. The plan of the erections is similar to those at Hegāratgi in all respects—that is, when open, three large slabs let into the ground, with a top-slab ; and when closed perfect in its four sides and cover. The dimensions of the largest were—

Side-slabs . . .	15 feet 3 inches long, each.
	9 feet 4 inches high, of which 3 feet, more or less, are let into the earth.
	8 to 10 inches thick.
Top	13 feet 9 inches long.
	13 feet broad.
	9 to 12 inches thick.
End-slab	6 feet broad.
	9 feet high, including what is in the ground.
	9 to 10 inches thick.

The interior of this cromlech measures more in length and breadth than the others, and is 6 feet by 9 ; but in others, and in the generality of the largest closed cromlechs or kistvaens, the interior space is 6 feet long by 4 broad, in which, as before stated, the funeral urns are depostied. A sketch of this cromlech is given in Pl. I, Figs. 3-4. The dimensions of two of the largest kistvaens are respectively :—

Side-slabs . . . 12 feet by 9.
Top . . . . 12 feet by 10 feet 6 inches.
9 to 12 inches thick.
Side-slabs . . . 12 feet 9 inches by 9 feet.
Top . . . . 13 feet 3 inches by 10 feet 9 inches.
1 foot to 9 inches thick.*

These two appear, one to the right and one to the left of Sketch No. 2, and that in the centre is about the same dimensions.† Sketch No. 3 shows some of the smaller kistvaens in another part of the ground, and No. 4 part of the group nearer the village of Rajan-Kolur. In this sketch the cromlech partly shown on the right hand is nearly, if not quite, as large as the largest of the main group, and is higher, but it is not so neatly constructed. Some of the others shown are partly open and broken, the sides and tops of some having fallen in, or been removed.

It is impossible to view these numerous remains without being impressed with a sense of the enormous labour required in their construction, and in the transport of such huge masses of heavy stone. The stone employed is a schistose grit or

* NOTE.—Compare the above dimensions with those of two cromlechs in the island of Anglesea, as quoted by Captain Congreve :—

"In the woods behind Plas Newydd, near the Menai Strait, are some very remarkable Druidical antiquities. Amongst them are two vast cromlechs. The upper stone of one is twelve feet seven inches long, twelve broad, and four thick supported by five tall stones. The other is but barely separated from the first, and is almost a square of five feet and a half, and supported by four stones. The number of supporters to cromlechs is merely accidental, and depends upon the size or form of the incumbent stone. These are the most magnificent we have, for a middle-sized horse may easily pass under the largest. In the woods of Llugwy. indeed, there is a most stupendous one of a rhomboidal form. The greatest diagonal is seventeen and a half feet, the lesser fifteen, and rhe thickness three feet nine inches, but its height from the ground is only two feet. It was supported by several stones. In the woods at this place are some Druidical circles nearly contiguous to each other."

The large Rajan-Kollur cromlech would, therefore, appear to be a finer specimen than either of these, which are, I believe, the largest in Great Britain ; the thickness of the upper slabs, in comparison with those of Rajan-Kollur, is the only superiority.

† The sketches referred to in this para. are not given in the *Journal*. But a plan of cromlechs, kistvaens, etc., is shown in Plate. IV.—G. Y.

sandstone, which occurs in a bed lying between the limestone bluffs above Rājan-Kollur and the granite ranges to the S. and SW., from half a mile to a mile, and a half broad. The bed, when nearest the granite, is very hard in texture, shows a strong lustre on fracture, as if it had been partially fused by heat, or granitized, and it is from these portions, which cannot be nearer than a mile and a half from the spot where the erections have been made, that the largest slabs have been raised and conveyed. The sand-stone changes its quality when not in contact with the granite, and is softer and more friable. It appears to resemble, if it be not identical with, the Bunter Sandstone, and is traversed by coloured bands—pink, grey, purple and yellow.

To have removed these masses at all must have required peculiar mechanical skill, as well as great application of force and labour; and their transport for so long a distance, and erection, particularly in the placing of the covering slabs, is almost unaccountable, with the means we may suppose a rude and pastoral people may have possessed. All things considered, this group is by far more remarkable than that of Hegaratgi, and in relation to the number and size of the cromlechs and kistvaens, may fairly take its place with the most remarkable of any of these remains hitherto discovered, whether in India or in Britain, France, Denmark, etc., None of the erections on the Nilgherris appear to approach them in size, and those opened by Captain Congreve agree with the dimensions of the middle and smaller sizes of the Rājan-Kollur and Hegaratgi groups. It will be observed by the plan that several cairns are intermingled with the stone erections, thus connecting the two as belonging to the same people. Several of these have double circles of stones, and have been carefully constructed; others are with single rows, and are less complete. I have not been able to examine any of these as yet, but I should presume, from trials elsewhere, that they would be found to contain funeral urns only ; and the ground on which they are is so hard, that as excavation of it to any depth would have been impossible, the urns have most likely been placed upon the rock, and covered with earth and loose stones, and have, therefore, most probably become decayed by the action of damp : it is only when they have been interred at a considerable depth from the surface that I have found them perfect. The whole of the ground covered by the erections is rock covered with a shallow surface of morum, into which the slabs have been fixed, resting upon the rock ; and this may account for the entire preservation of most of them. None of them, in the large group at least, appear to have been disturbed or examined at any time, and they are respected by the natives of the vicinity as the houses of the dwarfs, termed Morás, who inhabited the country in former ages before man. Locally they are known by the designation " Mora Mannee " or Morás' houses, but I have not been able to obtain any definition of the term " Morā." The main group stands on a slightly elevated spot with a gradual slope to the south, about half a mile SW. of Rājan-Kollur, and near the high road to Korikāl. The smaller group is nearer to the village, and adjoins the high road.

PLAN III.—CROMLECHS, ETC., NEAR BELSETTI-HAL.*

This village is situated about three miles NE. of Rājan-Kollur, on the high road to Shorapur, and the remains are near the range of limestone hills about half a mile WNW. of the village. There are very few of them entire, portions having been broken down and carried away, apparently for the slabs of stone ; others have fallen in. Some of them are small open cromlechs, and others kistvaens of the medium size of those at Rājan-Kollur, and none present any particular features for remark. The erections have not been arranged upon any plan,

* See Plate VII A.

but are scattered over in a long irregular line near the hills, and at their base. I did not think them of sufficient importance to have any opened or examined, but in respect to construction and appearance there is no difference between them and those at Rajan-Kollur. If possible, from their ruined condition, they may be more ancient than the others.

PLAN IV.—CAIRNS AT CHIKANHĀLLI. *

In the month of October 1851, when taking levels and surveys for the bund of a new tank near the village of Chikānhālli, which is about nine miles from Shorapur, on the road to Talikota, *via* Bohnal, I came very unexpectedly on a considerable group of cairns, which are situated on a small gravelly spur of a rock-granite range of hills about half a mile NW. from Chikanhalli. These cairns, large and small, are twelve in number, and are for the most part carefully constructed, with single and double rows of circle stones, and very perfect. The largest, on the summit of the elevation, had a treble row of stone round it, laid very regularly. The cairn was sixteen feet in diameter of the inner ring of stones, and, as I had remarked at Jiwarji and other places, the usual entrance stones at the SW. side were regularly placed, as also two stones NE. and SW., on the top of the tumulus. I had the large cairn on the summit of the knoll opened and examined. After digging a trench through loose stones and earth NE., and SW., in the direction of the top and entrance stones, beginning from the SW. entrance, to a level with the surrounding ground, or probably three feet, the lower excavation was carefully commenced from the same side. About four feet from the surface of the ground two large stones, or rough or irregular slabs, similarly placed to those in the cairns at Jiwarji, were met with, lying in the same direction as the entrance stones, but sloping and directing downwards. Following these, and

* Plan of these cairns is not published in the Journal.—G. Y.

at a depth of ten feet from the surface of the ground, some remains of pottery and bones were met with, and the excavation was continued to the bottom and around very carefully. The floor of the cairn consisted of slabs of stones, and was about five feet broad, and six feet long. On these a number of earthen pots or jars had been placed, of much larger size than any found at Jiwarji. Some of these were broken; some were too firmly inbedded in the earth and gravel of the sides of the cairn to be got out whole; but seven were recovered perfectly entire, or only slightly chipped, with their contents. The whole of the interior of the cairn was cleared out, until the natural gravelly walls of the excavation alone remained, but no traces of iron weapons, utensils, or small cups and urns, as at Jiwarji, were found. All the vessels got out whole had covers: they are of sound glazed pottery, of the same bright red colour as is generally met with, and, though not unlike the ordinary ghuras or chattees used by natives, are yet of peculiar and more elegant forms, the bottoms being more pointed. These pots contained portions of partly calcined human bones, ashes, and pieces of charcoal, mixed with earth, as in the kistvaens of Hegāratgi and Rājan-Kollur. The sides of the excavation were of strong morum or gravel; but the earth that had been filled in was soft, and without stones, and of the kind called "pandri mutti" by the natives, and must have been brought from some distance, as there is none anywhere near the spot. This earth had evidently been filled in after the urns had been deposited. It was impossible to ascertain how many had been originally deposited in the cairn, as so many broke on the earth being moved; but as well as I could estimate, there must have been at least from fifteen to twenty of various sizes, all having the same contents: those recovered were, however, the largest. I examined all the adjacent hills, in the hope of finding cromlechs or kistvaens, but without success, and I cannot hear of any other groups of cairns in this vicinity. I did not consider it necessary to open any more of the cairns, as it was evident that they belonged to the sect which burned their dead and buried their ashes only, without weapons, or smaller cups and utensils, and it is probable, I think, these cairns, which contain urns with ashes in them, belong to the same sect as those which used kistvaens for the same purpose, wherever stones could be conveniently obtained for their erection.

It is possible, also, that the cairns and kistvaens were family sepulchres, in which, as each member died in succession, his ashes were collected and deposited in the cairn. At the same time, the labour of opening out the whole, from top to bottom, on each successive occasion of a death, would have been almost equal to the construction of a new cairn; and if this system had been followed, a greater mixture of gravel of the soil of the spot with the soft whitish earth placed about the urns might have taken place, which would have been observable now. It is more probable, I think, that the cairns may have belonged to the tribe collectively; that as members died their ashes were preserved by their families in urns, and when a sufficient number had accumulated in the tribe they were deposited in a cairn, and finally closed up. This hypothesis appears, perhaps, more reasonable than the other; and may account as well for the perfect condition of these urn-cairns as for the manner in which the light earth was first placed, then covered by gravel and morum, and finally by stones and earth intermingled, to the top of the cairn, around which the double or single circles of large stones were placed.

REMAINS NEAR THE SHAHPUR HILLS.

These are of a very varied and interesting character, and it is necessary to describe them separately. The first met with, coming from Shorapur on the Shahpur road, about nine miles from Shorapur and three from Shahpur, is near the small village of Vaibāthālli, and lies immediately to the east of the high road, after passing the village in the direction of Shahpur. The road passes through a portion of it, so that the locality can easily be found. A plan of this curious spot is shown in Plates XV and XVI.

I presume it to have been ground regularly marked out for a cemetery of cairns, and the labour bestowed upon it has been enormous. The ground has been marked out in parallel or diagonal lines, leaving a square of from eighteen to twenty-four feet between each four points, which would be enough for an ordinary cairn; the points of the squares and the lines being formed of large granite rocks, which have evidently been rolled down the neighbouring hills, and placed in the situations they now occupy—but at what expense of labour, and with what patience! These rocks are irregular in shape, and of various sizes; but the average of them is not less than six to seven feet long by three to four thick or high, and very many are at least half as large again. The sides of the square, as it very nearly is, gave twenty rocks west, by twenty south, which, if the whole were complete, would amount to four hundred rocks; but a portion on the north-east corner and north side has not been completed, or the rocks have been removed, and about fifty would be required to complete the whole. Those laid down in the plan are from actual survey measurement, and the vacant spaces are as they exist. The whole of the ground is usually cultivated, but the size of the rocks has defied any attempt, if ever made, to remove any of them. I assume that the squares marked out must have been for cairns, as there are five,—two with double rows of stones, and three with single,—near the centre of the field, as shown in the plan; they are all very perfect, and have not been disturbed. The tradition attached to the spot is, that a king had once his encampment there, and the pieces of rocks were laid down for his horses and elephants. The place, therefore, in Canarese and Hindustani, is known by the name of "The King's Stables."

North of this field is another piece of cultivated ground, in which there are twenty-eight cairns, large and small—one with a triple circle of stones, which forms a considerable tumulus, two others with double circles, and the rest single. In one place four of the cairns are surrounded by what appears to have been a low wall, but most of the stones have been taken away, and as several of the cairns have evidently been broken by the plough, and the circle stones disturbed, it is possible that in the lapse of time, and constant cultivation of the field, many others may have been disturbed. Enough, however, remain to render the spot in connection with the rocks very remarkable and interesting. I was not able to have any of these cairns examined, but shall not fail to open the principal one and examine it the next time I am encamped near the spot.

PLAN VI. *

Is of a small group of cairns on a waste spot of ground below the tank of Amrāwätti, on the lands of Vaibathalli. There are five of them, one with a double circle of stones, the others with single. This group lies about a quarter of a mile W. or NW. of the preceding, and presents no particular features for remark.

PLAN VII. †

Is of a rather remarkable barrow or tumulus, and cairns, in a field on the lands of *Rakhamgira,* through which the high road from Shahpur to Saggi passes, and about a mile north of the last mentioned group. This tumulus has been formed with much care and labour, and though I tried to have a trench

* This plan is not given in the Journal.—G. Y.

† This plan is also not included.—G. Y.

dug through it, in order to ascertain its contents, the ground was so hard, and the moorum and stones had united into so strong a mass of concrete, that I was obliged to abandon it at the time, and have not been able to resume it. One of the cairns on the mound has a triple circle of stones, two double circles, and one single, and the whole of the mound is evidently artificial, the field around it being perfectly level. Originally there was one or more rows of stones all round the base, but these for the most part have been disturbed and removed. I have seen no tumulus so marked in character as this, in the Shorapur country, and on this account it merits more particular examination than I have been able to bestow upon it. In the same field are ten other cairns, eight in one group NW. of the large tumulus, and two by themselves SW. All these are insignificant in comparison with the others.

Not very far from the foregoing, perhaps a mile, and in the valley into which the road from Shahpur to Sāggi turns, is a remarkably large insulated granite rock, near a small rivulet which feeds the Amrawātti tank. This rock is about twenty feet high, and eight to ten yards in diameter, of a round irregular form. When I first saw it, it was surrounded by a double ring of large stones, very regularly placed, with two larger rocks as entrance on the south side; but the Wāddiwars employed in the repair of the tank have, I find, removed and displaced nearly all the circle stones. This rock, as I saw it first, had a very remarkable appearance, and impressed me with the belief that it must have been marked out as a place of worship or sacrifice. Captain Congreve, in his article before referred to, gives several instances of rocks on the Nilgherris as encircled by stones, and with which the one I mention exactly corresponded in all respects. I believe the same kind of Druidical remains is well known in Devonshire and in Cornwall, so that it is at least satisfactory to have found among the Shorapur remains one striking corroboration of identity with those of the Nilgherris and Britain, even in this particular.

PLAN VIII.*

This, as will be observed by the plan, is a smaller collection of rocks, in something the same plan as the larger one at Vaibāthālli. It is close to the hills, and upon the high road from Sāggi to Shahpur, near a small tank, and about a quarter of a mile from the large barrow. The rocks have not been completed to form exact squares in all instances, and, with a few exceptions, are not generally so large as those at Vaibathālli. Among them are two cairns, but of no remarkable size or construction.

Again, about a mile further north, and close to the eastern gate of the town of Shahpur, there is another group of lines of rocks similar to those already mentioned, which has once been as large, or nearly so, as that at Vaibāthālli; but the rocks placed here were, perhaps, for the most part of smaller sizes, and many have been removed, or are at least wanting; so that the lines are only perfect where they were too large to be stirred. Part of the space is a cultivated field, part is occupied by the high road, and the remainder is on waste ground to the east. As the lines of rocks were so imperfect, I did not survey the place, which is remarkable only in connection with the two others already mentioned. It could not, however, be overlooked by any one acquainted with the characters of these antiquities, as the rocks which remain have a very peculiar appearance in the ploughed ground, apparently so regular, and where, except these, are no others of any

* Plan is not given in the Journal—G. Y.

description. I could not find traces of cairns among these rocks; if there were any originally, they have been long ago obliterated by the cultivation of the greater portion of the land in which they are, and which is of excellent quality.

PLAN IX.—TUMULUS AND ROCKS NORTH OF THE SHAHPUR HILLS.*

I consider this as by far the most remarkable of the remains about Shahpur, if, indeed, it does not much exceed in interest even the cromlechs, in the enormous labour with which the outer lines of rocks have been placed as they are. I had no idea of its existence until one day when encamped at Shahpur, in June last year, and having to examine a well near a temple which required repair, I came upon the tumulus quite by accident, as I was riding across the fields. It transpired, however, that the place was well known to the people, who have a legend regarding it, which was told me by my companion, the Pujári of the temple, to this effect:—Once upon a time a party of Bedins had brought up a large spoil of cattle and goats from a neighbouring district, and on their return quarrelled about the division of the booty. As they happened at the time not to be far from the temple of Amlapur Hanuman, which is held very sacred among these people, and it was near day, they agreed to stop and ask the opinion of the god as to what they shuold do. The cattle, therefore, were collected in a group,—the bullocks and buffaloes outside, the cows and calves next, and the sheep and goats in the centre,—and all lay down to rest. When day dawned, the thieves went to the temple, which is hard by, and alone in the plain; and having reminded the god of sundry offerings to him before they set out on their raid, to which and to his favour they were indebted for a successful foray, they stated that, try as they would, they could not bring themselves to a conclusion as to the disposal of the proceeds; and, though loth to trouble him,

* Please see Plate XV.

begged him to step down to where the cattle lay, and decide the quarrel, or it would end in all of them fighting among themselves and being slain, which would bring great discredit upon him. The god was willing to be arbitrator, got off his pedestal, and proceeded as he was to the place where the cattle stood, and, having selected some good cows and buffaloes for the Brahmins of the temple, proceeded to divide the rest according to his notions of justice. This, however, was by no means so easy as he supposed : he was accused by all the thieves of favoritism, and that because such a man had made a sacrifice on such a day, and another had not ; a third had a vow to fulfil, and another had made none ; he was evidently prepossessed in favour of his votaries, and could not be a judge at all—so the best way, as they had at first proposed, was to settle the quarrel by the sword, and whoever should be victorious in the end was to take all. Upon this the god fell into great wrath, declared his reputation would be ruined forever if a parcel of roving Bedins came and fought in his holy precincts, under his very nose ; and after (according to my informant) a liberal abuse of the female relatives of the party, declared not a beast should move. Gradually, then, and to the horror of the Bedins, the cattle sunk down motionless, and became stone. The Pujári, when he had got thus far in his story, triumphantly exclaimed—" There ! you see the truth of the story verified ; for see, the sheep are all black, and the other cattle grey, and of all colours, stricken as they lay ! " I ventured to remark that some of the rocks were very tall for cows and buffaloes. " Ah, " said he, " that's true ; but you forget that men were giants in those days, and so their cattle were large too ; we are pigmies now in comparison ; "—and as he seemed quite satisfied with his own conclusions, it was no use to gainsay them. The stones are therefore considered as a proof of the miraculous power of the Amlapur

Hanuman, though the Bedins hint that it was a spiteful trick of the god to turn so many good beasts into stone for such a trifle as a few lives.

It was at once, however, very evident what the stones were, and a very striking appearance have they in the wide plain when the ground is clear of crops. A long and correctly formed parallelogram of 400 feet by 260; composed of huge masses of granite, encloses a smaller figure of smaller rocks, and these a tumulus rising about ten feet above the surrounding ground. The circle of stones at the summit was of superior diameter to any I had seen; the sides of the tumulus were covered with large black rocks of greenstone, and these surrounded on three sides by a double row, and to the east by six rows of granite rock, partly incomplete, and of smaller size. The tumulus measured sixty feet in diameter between the circle of stones on the summit, which was bare and level; the slope southwards and eastwards from the west, as the ground has a natural inclination to the south, was sixty feet; and that on the north and west, where the ground rose, was forty feet. On the slopes of the SW. and NE. corners were two other smaller circles of black stones, of smaller diameter; and the rest of the greenstone rocks had been placed, apparently without regular design, so as to cover the whole of the slopes on all sides, the parallelogram enclosed by them being 190 feet north and south, by 160 feet east and west. The exact number of these black rocks it was impossible to ascertain correctly as also the positions of all; and after several attempts to have them corrected, and to lay them down correctly, I was obliged, for want of time, to give the matter up, and to judge as far as possible by my eyes, counting and measuring the outside lines, and counting and filling up the rest by portions as they appeared to lie. The inner lines of granite rocks, and those of the main outer line of the parallelogram, were carefully counted and measured, and laid down in the plan by observation, in their proper positions, and with reference to the scale of forty feet to an inch. I extract from my field-book the measurements of some of the largest rocks of the outside lines. It would be tedious and unnecessary, perhaps, to give the whole:—

	Length		Breadth		Height		Girth	
	ft.	in.	ft.	in.	ft.	in.	ft.	in
Rock	10	5	7	4	5	1	26	9
,,	9	0	8	0	4	3	24	6
,,	10	1	9	7	5	2	27	9
,,	7	2	4	3	4	0	24	3
,,	3	6	8	2	6	8	26	3
,,	9	0	5	6	7	3	25	6
,,	9	0	4	3	8	9	21	0
,,	7	6	8	1	3	8½	24	9
,,	9	0	7	6	5	0	20	9
,,	9	5	8	4	5	8	27	2

The weight of each might be computed, but I have not attempted it. The rest are but little short of these dimensions, varying from 8 feet 4 inches long, 6 feet broad, and 4 feet high, to 6 feet long, 5½ feet broad, and 3 feet 9 inches high, which is the smallest of any. How these rocks were moved, and placed as they are, so regularly, it is impossible to conceive. The nearest granite rocks are those on the hills of the Shahpur range, which, opposite to the tumulus, is quite a mile and a half distant, and there are no others anywhere in the plains for miles around. The geological character, indeed, of the country, changes after leaving the hills, and the limestone formation commences. I can, therefore, come to no conclusion but that the rocks, which are identical in character with those of the Shahpur range, were rolled down from them into the plain, and from thence rolled, or otherwise conveyed onwards to their destination. The removal of one of these masses of granite would be an almost impossible undertaking with the means at present obtainable in the country; and yet there are fifty-six placed here, all of which have been brought from the hills across two nullas, one of which has rather steep banks, at least fifteen feet deep, of soft earth—a serious obstacle. Great as has been the labour to transport and erect the slabs of sandstone and limestone of which the cromlechs and kistvaens of Rajan-Kollur and Hegaratgi are constructed, the means employed there sink into insignificance when compared with the transport of these great rocks. How many men were employed in the undertaking—how much time—what mechanical or other means—it is impossible to conjecture; but they stand, monuments of the faith of bygone ages, alike immovable and imperishable. Sketches Nos. 12 and 13 (Pl. XV) will give, perhaps, a better idea of them than any description. No. 13 shows the south side, and No. 12 the east, in which the largest rocks are situated, and are as correct as to shape and situation as I could make them. The greenstone rocks in the slope of the tumulus are no less worthy of remark, and their great weight for their size, and the distance from which they have been brought, evince the patience and perseverance of the people who transported them. Generally speaking, these are from four to six feet long, and from two to three feet broad and high, mostly of an irregular round figure. The nearest bed or dyke of greenstone rocks among the granite hills is about five miles from the tumulus, to the SW., and these rocks must, therefore, have been brought from thence, either upon carts, or rolled or carried by men. The former supposition is, perhaps, the most probable, as these people may have had rude cars, such as are now used by the Wāddiwars or stone-workers of the country; many of the rocks are, however, too large to be transported by these means.

Having completed my survey, I proceeded to ascertain the contents of the tumulus, and directed two trenches to be cut through the mound, one north and south, A to B, the other east and west, C to D. These trenches were six feet wide, and were begun from the natural ground, so that the contents of the mound would, I trusted, fully appear. Nothing, however, was found in the shape of the remains of urns, weapons, or cists, as in others. A few pieces of broken pottery were found now and then, but nothing worth preserving. Where the trenches crossed each other the excavation was continued to some depth, but without success, the morum being hard and compact, and had evidently never been disturbed. The trenches ultimately gave sufficient clue to the object and construction of the tumulus; for layer after layer of ashes, partially burnt bones, and bits of charcoal, and earth and sand burned or run into slag, as it were by the action of fire, proved that successive cremations had taken place in great numbers, down to the floor of the ground. It was evident that as a body was burned, the spot had been covered over with soft greyish earth,—*pandri mutti,*—and the tumulus had risen by a succession of these layers, which were in some places five and six in number, all of the same character.

It is possible, therefore, that this spot was the place where all the dead of the tribe were burned; that their ashes were collected in part, and removed to be buried in cairns, as at Chikānhālli; and that when the tribe migrated the tumulus was completed, and finally sealed and secured by its circle of stones on the slopes as I have described; or it may have been, that on the death of a great chief many persons were sacrificed, their bodies burned, and the tumulus constructed at once. The great number of indications of one body having been burned on each spot, and the successive layers of fresh earth and ashes, with burned earth and slag, incline me more to the former supposition than the latter; and, as far as I could ascertain from the trenches, which laid bare the whole of the interior by sections of nine feet deep at the crest of the mound, and six broad, there seemed to be no portion of it, including the slopes, which were free from the indications I have already noticed. It is evident, not only from the labour bestowed upon the tumulus, but from the remains at Vaibathälli, Rakhämgira, and Shahpur, all on the east side of the hills, as well as those on the north, that there must have been a large encampment or settlement of these people about Shahpur. I have looked in vain, however, for any traces of ancient walls, or indications of habitations, if I may except one doubtful spot, not far from the rock which had circles of stones round it, and which shows some traces of old walls, as well as small pieces of red glazed pottery. The Shahpur range is a mass of granite, 700 to 1,000 feet high above the plain, intersected by deep ravines, and very rocky. I thought it probable, perhaps, that cairns or cromlechs might be found on the summit plateau, which is some miles in extent; but the parties I sent could find nothing, and I was not able to examine the hills myself. I am not aware that there are any other remains in the vicinity of Shahpur but those I have described.

PLAN X.—ROCKS AND CAIRNS AT IJÈRI.*

A group of trap rocks, which have been placed in the same manner, and apparently with the same intention, as those near Shahpur, lies upon a rising ground about a mile west of the village of Ijèri, of the Nellugi talook. A few rocks are wanting to complete the squares, but the arrangement is obviously regular, and some of the rocks are of large size,—eight to ten feet long, four to six feet broad, and three to four feet thick,—and, from the nature of the stone, very heavy. The rocks have been brought a mile and a half or two miles,

* Plan is not published in the Journal.—G. Y.

from the ravines to the north or west. There are two cairns among this group, each occupying the area of a square. but they did not appear of sufficient consequence to have opened. South-west of the same village, about half a mile on the road to Bālbatti, there are three other cairns, one of large size, of which the circle of stones is double ; the other two are of smaller dimensions, and have only single circles. The village of Ijêri is situated about eighteen miles to the NW. of Shahpur. I have not been able to discover any of these or other Druidic antiquities in the intermediate line of villages, nor in any of those immediately around it ; but it is evident that there was an encampment here, and, as the ravines abound with grass and water, large herds of cattle would have found ample sustenance.

PLAN XI.—CAIRNS AT MANDEWALLI.*

This village belongs to the same talook as the preceding, and is situated about the centre of it, about twelve miles NW from Ijéri. In the month of February of the present year, as I was travelling from Almella, in the British territory, to Ijèri, I passed these remarkable remains, which are situated about a mile NW. of Māndewalli, on the Jeritgi road, on a rising ground of hard morum and rock, covered with large trap rocks. Among these the four principal platforms are very distinct, and have been constructed with immense labour and patience. They consist of double and treble rows of large rocks, joining each other, surrounded by a square of rocks of similar size, the intervals being filled up with smaller rocks, placed so as to touch each other in most instances, and forming a complete and almost impenetrable covering to the ground beneath, which rises to the apex of the cairn, where from four to six rocks have been placed together as a seal to the whole. Part of the largest cairn is incomplete,

* Plan is not published in the Journal.—G. Y.

the cultivation having gradually encroached upon it, and the rocks being scattered about. Between the three large platforms and the single one to the north there are two small cairns, no way remarkable, and to the right of the road to Māndewalli six other cairns in a group, on an open gravelly spot. These present no particular features for remark, and seem in every respect the same as those noticed in other places. I did not halt at Mandewalli, but as soon as possible sent a party of men with a Karkoon to open one of these remarkable cairns; but they returned in a few days, saying that it was impossible to remove the masses of rock, which, one over the other, were tightly jammed together. A few pieces of pottery were found, broken urns, which showed the platforms to be true cairns; but whether pertaining to a tribe which buried or burned its dead, complete investigation could alone determine. It is probable that other cairns may be found on the lands of this village, and in the purgunna, particularly on the slopes of, and among the grassy ravines which descend from the high land about Ijeri and other villages on the plateau, and I purpose, if possible, to renew my examination this year.

PLAN XII.—CAIRNS AT JIWÂRJI.*

I now return to the village, the remains at which were the subject of my first communication to the Society. The plan sent will give an exact idea of the situation of the cairns, and their number, the whole having been carefully surveyed by me, and Sketch No. 3 (Pl. VIII) of the general appearance of the ground. There are 268 cairns in all, small and large: the plan distinguishes those which have single and double rows of stones round them, as well as those which I have opened, and those which, composed of slabs of limestone placed parallel to each other, are, as it were, square or oblong open cists, and in which, except a few potsherds, every remnant of former

* See Plates VIII and IX.—G. Y.

deposit seems to have disappeared. To the south of the cairns, near the banks of the Jiwarji nulla, are the evident remains of a small village; foundations of walls built of stones and mud; heaps of mounds; and in every direction portions, small and large, of the same red glazed pottery as is dug out of the cairns, are lying about, as also in a field adjoining, where they are turned up by the plough. I cannot, therefore, refuse to consider that this may have been the Scythic village whose inhabitants were, perhaps, with others from surrounding camps, buried in the cairns; without, indeed, it was merely the place where pottery was made, and which may have required roofed houses for drying and manufacture. It would be desirable to have trenches dug through some of the ruined mounds; and should I visit Jiwarji this year, I will endeavour to have this done.

In April and May I was so severely indisposed that I could not effect so much as I wished in the way of examination of cairns; but in all four large ones were opened, and several smaller cists, square and oblong, and I proceed to detail what appears most remarkable in the examination.

In one of the large cairns there were two regular cists, or stone coffins, one of which, on the east side, contained one skeleton, the other, on the west side, two, of which *one skull only* was in the cist. The whole of these skeletons were perfect enough to have shown the missing skull if it had been placed anywhere in the cist, or had been on the body; and one of the two skeletons in the west cist had a head; the other had two of the neck vertebræ attached to the spine, which may favour the supposition that the body—apparently that of a woman, from the smallness of the bones—had been beheaded. Above the cist, and met with as the excavation continued from above, were distinct remains of four other bodies and skulls, with smaller bones, and portions of a few skulls of children. The remains of the bodies were by no means regularly disposed; indeed, from the positions of the bones, they seemed to have been pitched into the grave at random, one over another. None of the skulls were found attached to the bodies, or in the places they ought to have occupied in the earth if the bodies had been interred whole, but were found confusedly here and there, without any reference to the skeletons. This cairn contained comparatively few urns or pots, and no remnants of weapons could be found, beyond a few undistinguishable portions of iron, completely corroded. The most perfect skeleton in the cist to the east was five feet two inches long, and was that of a male adult; the others did not appear to me to be as much as five feet, but they were so confused that I could not make any satisfactory measurements.

The other large cairn, which indeed is a considerable tumulus, near the centre of the group, was of the usual depth, that is eleven feet from the crest of the mound, and contained a large cist four feet ten inches long inside, by three feet broad; and was formed into two divisions by a slab of limestone, lengthways; the divisions being, respectively, to the east two feet broad, and to the west one foot. There were two skeletons in the larger portion of the cist, laid over each other, the upper one *face downwards*, the other and lower one on its side, the heads of which were properly attached to the spine; but on the top of these heads, and so discovered before the bodies below, a skull was placed *upright* in the middle by itself, with vertebræ attached to it. This skull was nearly whole when got out, but the dry hot winds caused it to crumble away almost entirely in the course of the day, which I much regretted. The cover of this cist was nearly perfect, only one slab, towards the feet of the skeletons, having fallen in, so that it is impossible that any skull could have fallen down through the earth to the bodies below. In the cist, therefore, were two skeletons, placed as I have described, with an *extra skull*, evidently placed where it was found after the bodies had been deposited. The portion of the cist one foot broad contained urns and pots filled with earth only, some of which—the small ones inside larger ones—were very perfect. Of the large ones none came out entire, and the remains of an iron knife and a spear-head were among the urns, some of which, with the spear-head, were sent to the Society.

Now the excavation had been most carefully carried down in my presence after the first bones were met with, for I wished much to have further proof that persons had been beheaded and interred—in other words that human sacrifices had been made. From time to time bones were met with, but very irregularly, and much decayed. Two skulls were found, but not with other bones, nor with spinal vertebræ. It was impossible to judge exactly how many bodies were interred there, but I should think five or six adults, independent of those in the cist that I have now to make more particular mention of. The whole of the upper earth had been taken up as far as the covering slabs of the cist, and thrown out of the grave, except a portion over the head of the cist. On breaking into this, bones were found, and the earth then carefully picked away from them. Tracing and exposing them, the result was the disclosure of a skeleton lying transversely, that is east and west, on the lid of cist, and lying upon it. The body was headless; but after a little more search the skull, at the time nearly perfect, was found, as it had evidently been placed, in the centre of the body, and resting upon the pelvic bones. The skull was upright, and looked to the south. It was so entire that I wished to take it to my tent to draw it at leisure, but on attempting very gently to remove it, it fell to pieces in my hands.

I was too ill when the other two cairns were opened to examine their contents as I had done these, but my people, now accustomed to observe, told me that on the floor of one cairn (it had no cist) there were three skeletons, lying north and south, and four skulls, and that bones had been met with confusedly, as the digging descended, with portions of skulls; and that there were only a few pots, none of which came out whole. In the other, also without a cist, there was only one skeleton on the floor of the grave, with a few pots to the west of it, at the usual depth; and that very few bones, and only one skull, had been met with as the excavation proceeded.

I have before stated that none of the open cists yielded anything, though one was exceedingly promising in appearance. It was composed of four large slabs of limestone let into the earth to within a foot of the surface; in fact, not unlike a large cromlech or kistvaen, let down till nearly covered, but without a top. The sides were eight feet six inches long by five feet eight inches broad; the ends five feet broad by five feet six inches high. The interior contained nothing whatever that could be distinguished, beyond a few broken potsherds, and some much decayed pieces of bone. None of the smaller cists, of which several were examined, yielded anything. In all these cairns precisely the same method of construction as described in my last communication was found to exist; *1st*, the circle of stones; *2nd*, the tumulus within them, composed of loose stones and earth; *3rd*, the entrance stones, laid NE. and SW. Then, on digging down from the entrance stones, the two other large slabs were found, leading to the foot of the cist; next, the cist, at a depth of from eleven to fourteen feet from the surface, and eight to ten feet from the bottom of the upper entrance stones, the body of the grave being filled with fine earth, without stones. No one passing from the Bhima at Ferozabad to Jiwarji by the high road can possibly miss this interesting group of remains; and it is well worth the while of any traveller to turn aside from the road to examine the spot. It is easily found by an old Mahomedan tomb and a single tree by which the road passes, and on the left of the road as you go to Jiwarji, and opposite to the tomb, are black trap circles of large stones, which are the cairns.

PLAN XIII.—CAIRNS ON THE LANDS OF ANDOLA.*

I had discovered this group of cairns the year before, but had not been able to examine any of them. They occupy a small elevation immediately to the right of the road leading from Chārmur to Andola, about half way distant, or a mile and a half from each village. They are about five miles SE. of the Jiwarji cemetery. The elevation they are upon is waste, and is composed of limestone shale, harder than that at Jiwarji, slightly covered with dark coloured earth. In all there are forty cairns and cists distinguishable, but the villagers informed me that the ground had been formerly cultivated in parts, and it is probable some of the smaller cairns may have been obliterated, especially on the ground to the W. and NW., which is softer, and the soil deeper than that on the crest of the ridge. In appearance these cairns are precisely the same as those at Jiwarji, the circles of stones, double and single, being carefully placed, with the entrance stones in several above the ground : one cist, of slabs of limestone let into the earth, is eight feet long by four wide ; the rest are smaller, and appear to be graves of children. I had two of these cairns opened with considerable labour and trouble, for the surface stones and portions of shale had become so hard, that it was with great difficulty that the workmen could break through them with the pickaxe. Those selected were the largest of the main group on the summit of the ridge, and were eighteen feet in diameter inside the circles of stones, had large entrance stones, and were in every respect complete and undisturbed. I give in Plan XIV.† sections of both of these graves.

* See Plate XII.—G.Y.

† Plan not published in the Journal.—G.Y.

No. I was the first opened at the entrance stones. As the excavation proceeded, a great quantity of bones, large and small, were found in the softer earth below the upper concrete, and several portions of skulls. I was present at part of this examination, and nothing could have been more confused than the appearance of the bones lying in all possible directions. For the most part they were harder, and in better preservation than the bones usually found, but very brittle; and as there was no apparent guide from their positions to the positions of the skeletons, there were none found as perfect as I could have wished. I observed, however, here, as at Jiwarji, that there was no apparent relation of the skulls when found to the bones of the skeletons, except in one instance, where the bones led to the position of the skull, and the body had evidently been laid down in the proper line of the cist: this was immediately over the cist, and resting upon it. Above this, some skulls were found towards the foot of the grave, to the SW., others in the opposite direction, among the earth; but with the exception of the one I have mentioned above, *not one* in connection with the skeleton bones. Remains of eight skulls were found in this portion of the grave. The cist of this cairn was very perfect, and lay ENE. and WSW. by compass, and was made of slabs of limestone, five placed transversely as a floor, neatly joined with single slabs for sides 5 feet 6 inches long, and 1 foot 9 inches high. The slabs are 2 inches thick. The head and foot slabs were 6 feet long by 1 foot 9 inches high, and the whole was divided into two equal portions or cists 3 feet wide. The covering slabs were all perfect, except one at the foot, which had broken and fallen in. On removing these the cists were found to contain two skeletons each, those to the east being of a larger size than any I had yet seen, and fully filling the cist: they had been laid as nearly as possible one over another, and were apparently perfect. Those on the west side were smaller and more decayed, but the skulls were in their proper places: from the smallness of the bones I supposed them to be of women. Again, to the west of the cist, and between it and the natural wall or side of the grave, were many remains of human bones, for the most part small and delicate, apparently those of children, with several remains of their skulls; but it was impossible, from the decay of all, to trace the skulls to the skeletons. A few pots were found at the head and on the west side of the cist, large and small, and some perfect but in nowise different from those of the Jiwarji cairns, either in shape or colour.

Cairn No. 2 was eighteen feet broad inside the circle. The excavation proceeded as in the one preceding, but an attack of fever prevented my seeing it. My people, however reported it to be exactly similar to the preceding one; that bones were found lying in all directions, some transversely, some diagonally and some direct, with portions of skulls here and there confusedly. The remains of five skulls, with portions of leg, thigh, and arm bones, and some vertebræ, were brought to me, but all broken in removal.

I had directed the cist to be reserved for my own inspection, and as soon as I could, went to see it. I found it entirely perfect, none of the cover having fallen in. On removing the upper slabs, the cist appeared divided into two portions; the one to the east being 5 feet 6 inches long by 2 feet 2 inches broad. The other to the west was 1 foot 2 inches broad by 5 feet 6 inches long, and there were slabs for the floor. In the eastern, or larger cist, was one skeleton only, which was very distinctly traceable from the feet upwards, the smaller bones being distinguishable, though they crumbled immediately, as also the pelvic bones and vertebræ. I trusted, therefore, to find the skull at least perfect, and attached to the skeleton, but to my surprise, on reaching it, I found it separate from the body, and lying with the face to the NE. corner of the cist, and the top of the cranium to the SW. part of the skull rested upon the bone and shoulder of the left arm. It is not very possible that the head could have got into the position it was by the body having been interred upon its belly, which I have found the case in some instances, though not many, as then the jaws would have been towards the body ; whereas the whole was entirely reversed, and must have been placed separate from the body. The plan of the cist. (No. 17) gives the exact position of the head as it lay, and Sketch No. 8 its size and shape, traced without removing it.* The measurements round the head were as follows :—

	ft.	in.
From feet of skeleton to SW. side of skull or top of cranium	3	6
From head stone inside to NE. side of jaws and neck ..	1	7
From face to west side of cist or middle slab ..	1	5
From back of skull to east slab	0	5

Some urns and pots were found, as usual, upon the west side of the cist, most of which were broken in removal, and a few pieces of iron much decayed. On a small shelf, however, of the side of the cairn, in a hollow which had been made for it, an urn in perfect preservation was found, which contained no earth, and only some light dust, with some bones, very white and delicate, which I conjectured to be those of a mungoose. These, with other bones, were sent by me to Dr. Carter, the Secretary of the Society, with some specimens of pottery found in the cairns. He informed me, in acknowledgment of the several articles, that the small bones were those of a guana, and that a portion of the jawbone of a canine animal, probably a dog, had been found with the other bones. This was the only instance in which I had met with such remains, and the pot or urn in which they had been

* The plan and the sketch mentioned here are not published in the Journal.—G.Y.

placed had evidently been put aside with care. I had purposed to open another of these cairns,—that on the crest of the rise near the small nulla, which is perfect, and had double rows of circle stones,—but I was obliged to leave Jiwarji from continued illness, and the work was not commenced.

Enough, however, in relation to my former communication, has, perhaps, been stated, to show the contents and construction of these very ancient graves, and to establish their identity with other Celtic-Scythian graves and cairns elsewhere examined in India, as well as in Europe. Nor can there, I think, be any room to doubt that human sacrifices, as I ventured to suggest in my last paper, in reference to the position of the skull, which was then described as found by itself among the urns at the head of a cist, took place to a considerable extent when a body or bodies were buried. The positions of skeletons without heads, lying in all directions, as if confusedly flung into the graves ; the positions of skulls found without reference to skeletons ; the very remarkable instances in the Jiwarji cairns of a skull being found inside a perfect cist placed upright between those of two skeletons ; and of a skeleton being found lying transversely across the cover of the cist without a skull, the skull itself having been placed upright, and upon the middle or pelvic bones, with the face to the south—all serve to impress me with the conviction that the bodies so found were those of human victims. Whether the skeletons decapitated were those of women or men. I regret I have not sufficient anatomical knowledge to determine. Captain Congreve, in his most valuable article, quoting from Herodotus in Melpomene, recounting the funeral of a Scythian king, states that " after the body has been transported through the various provinces of the kingdom, it is placed on a couch set round by spears. His concubines are then sacrificed, and a mound of earth is raised over the king and his women."*

* Vide extract from Rollin's *Ancient History* at conclusion.

Other works upon this subject might probably afford details of Scythic or Celto-Druidic customs in this respect, and of human sacrifices, probably of both men and women, slaves, captives, and concubines ; but I regret I have none to refer to. Captain Congreve mentions, however, the sacrifice of children by the Scythians, and Thautawars of the Nilgherris ; and in these cairns the bones of children are found with the others interred in the graves, while in some they have been burned and placed in urns. May we suppose, therefore, that children, as well as men and women, were sacrificed in funeral ceremonies ?

In respect of the funeral urns or pottery, the forms of those which I have recovered here are simpler, probably from their greater antiquity, than those found on the Nilgherris, and are generally or for the most part without ornament. The material appears to be the same. I have no work to refer to by me in which I could compare the shapes of the urns and cups found here with those of Europe ; but I see that they are in some instances identical with several given in a description of the " Kodey Kulls or Pandoo Koolies," at Chataperambah, on the Beypoor river, in Malabar, by J. Babington, Esq., (*Transactions of the Literary Society of Bombay,* vol. iii, 1820); and that the iron instruments—an iron tripod, a spoon lamp, spear-heads, etc., are also identical with others found here in cairns, not of precisely the same construction, but agreeing in general principles.

At the village of Kolur, of the Andola talook, about four miles due north of Jiwarji, there are the remains of six large cairns on an elevation near the bank of the river Bhima, which are surrounded by single and double circles of trap rocks, like those at Jiwarji. They are in one line north and south, at the interval of a few yards from each other, and, being of the same construction, present no particular features for remark. I was not able to have any of these opened. These are the last cairns I had found to the northwards, and though I had made repeated inquiries from the native authorities of the Gulburgah district, I have not been able to discover any Scythic remains north of the Bhima in this direction.

CHAPTER II

Having detailed all the remains I have as yet found in the Shorapur district, I now pass to notices of such remains in other districts, which have been kindly supplied to me by friends who have observed them. The first are from the letters of the Revd. G. Keis, German Missionary at Bettigherri, in the Dharwar Collectorate, to whom I showed some of the Shorapur remains, cromlechs as well as cairns, and who thus became familiar with their appearance.

PLAN XIV.—CROMLECHS, ETC., NEAR KOSGI.*

The town of Kosgi is situated about nine miles south of the Tungabhadra, and eighteen miles north of Adwani, in the Bellary Collectorate. The cromlechs lie in a corner formed by three hills, joining each other about one mile south of the town. Nos. 1 and 2 are closed erections (kistvaen); No. 1 has a circular opening in the southern slab, as also has No. 2. The dimensions of the interior are in both instances 6 feet high, 5 feet long, and 4 to 4½ feet broad. Both erections stand on the solid rock, without any covering of earth upon them. No. 2 has a pavement slab, 4½ feet long and 3½ feet broad, so that an empty space of 6 inches broad remains on the eastern and northern sides, filled up with fragments of stone and rubbish. This I searched all through, but could find nothing, except small fragments of red and black pottery, a small piece of kindled wood, and a piece of bone, apparently of the skull of an animal, and not burned. No. 3 opens to the south, is of somewhat larger dimensions, and stands also on the solid naked rock. I searched in vain for anything in it.

* Plan not published in the Journal.—G. Y.

No. 4 is a smaller erection, more than half buried in the earth. Its dimensions within are 3 feet from north to south, 3½ feet broad from west to east, and 4 feet high. The southern slab is not pressed by the side slabs, nor by the covering slab, so that it could easily be taken out if the earth were removed. The inner space was filled up with earth, of which the upper third, that is so much as is above the ground surrounding the erection, seems to have been filled up by ants. I could not see any remains of pottery, or indeed of anything whatever. There are a number of similar erections round No. 4. Some of them have still the covering slab on them, and others not. As a characteristic distinction of these erections it appeared to me that the side-slabs are much thinner than those of Numbers 1, 2, 3, 4, and 5; that two-thirds of them are buried in the ground, but they always present the form

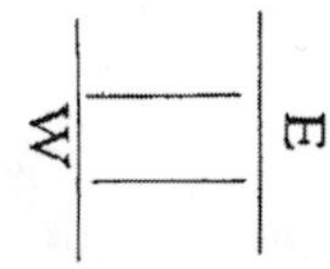

and never

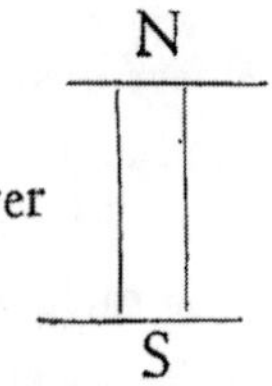

; and that their greatest dimensions are not from one cross-slab to the other, as in Nos. 1, 2, 3, but from one side-slab to the other.

No. 5 are remains of erections similar to Nos. 1, 2, 3, tumbled to pieces. It does not appear to me that any of them ever contained anything. No. 6 are segments of single and double circular rows of stones, of which the uppermost parts appear above the ground. It seemed to me as if the different segments were not the fragments of one large circle, but of several smaller ones. The space within these circles, and around and along No. 4, and the fragments about it, is the only spot where the solid rock has a covering of earth, which in the middle may be 5 to 6 feet in thickness.

The hypothesis which suggested itself to me in consideration of the actual observation on the spot was, that Nos. 1, 2, 3, and 5, were small houses of a nomadic tribe, whilst Nos. 4 and 6 were their burying-places—No. 4, one-third above the ground, because it was not deep enough, and No. 6, in the midst of those circles of tombs similar to No. 4, all covered with earth where it was deep enough.

PLAN XV.—CROMLECHS NEAR YEMMI GUDA.*

From Hampi, (Beejanugger) I crossed the Tungabhadra opposite Anagundi, from which place I went in the direction of Yemmi Guda (the hill of the buffaloes), and arrived that evening at Mallapur, about four miles north, or rather NNW. from Anagundi. I asked the Patel for the "dwarf houses" at or near Yemmi Guda : he told me that there was a whole village of them on the top of a high hill just midway between Mallapur and Yemmi Guda, that is about four miles north of Mallapur, and four to five miles SE. from Yemmi Guda ; and that he had heard of dwarf houses in the immediate neighbourhood of the latter place, while the dwarf houses were known to all the neighbouring villages. So I concluded this to be the settlement of which you were told by the Kanacgiri man. Next morning I went with the Patel and some other persons, and, after a good deal of strolling about, we succeeded in finding the dwarf village, and I refer you to the sketch and description.

Near Mallapur itself, on the side of the valley, is another settlement. The remains of some twenty to thirty erections and graves are to be seen, but none of them preserved wholly. Of a third settlement, with a number of erections still standing, I heard, on the right bank of the Tungabhadra, about five miles SW. from Anagundi. I have now not the least doubt, that

* See Plate VII B.—G. Y.

f properly searched, such settlements would be found scattered here and there over the whole of the Deccan and Southern India in all the hilly parts ; and equally certain it appears to me, after having seen the settlements at Kosgi and Yemmi Guda, that the large erections, open and closed, were houses, and not tombs ; but that the tombs are separate from them, and differ in size and structure from the houses. I only beg you to re-examine the settlement at Rajan-Kollur after you have read this, in order to find out whether, on closer examination, it does not agree with my observations and hypothesis.

Altogether in this place, including those that are still standing, and those that are fallen, the remains may amount to nearly a hundred, and they lie about in the utmost irregularity between the granite rocks. The direction from north to south predominates, but there are erections in every direction, as the plan shows, the most part of which was sketched from actual observation. The circular opening in the middle of one of the slabs is irregular, and its corners in some of them are as irregularly situated as possible. Preference seems to have been given to no particular quarter of the heavens, as the plan shows, in which the dot indicates the form and direction of the opening, taken by actual observation. The dimensions of the erections differ considerably : Nos. 1, 2, and 3 were measured. Of No. 1, the side-slabs are 9 feet long, and 6 feet 5 inches high, and the cross-slab 7 feet broad by 9 feet long. No. 2 is also an open house, almost of the same size. No. 3 is a closed one 8 feet 5 inches long, 8 feet 5 inches high, and 6 feet 5 inches broad. No. 1, as well as many other erections, closed and open, has a circular wall round it 2½ feet high, 4 feet broad, and 5 feet distant from the corners of the erection. All closed erections have a slab for the pavement or floor, and all are erected on the naked solid rock. In none of them could I find any remains, as of pottery, etc.

On it I measured Nos. 1, 2, 3, 4, and 5. No. 1 is a triple tomb, 7 feet long within, and each space between the slabs 3 feet broad, exactly corresponding with the size of a full-grown body, with some inches left all around. No. 2 measures within 5 feet 5 inches long, and each of the spaces 2 feet broad. No. 3 is evidently the tomb of a child, 3 feet long, and 1 foot broad. No. 4 a double tomb, 6 feet 5 inches long, and 2 feet broad each. No. 5 a double tomb, 7 feet long, and 2 feet broad. Both spaces are covered by one large slab. On No. 1 are two separate slabs. I saw no circular sepulchral cairns like those in the Shorapur country.

The whole settlement lies on the top of a granite hill about 500 to 600 feet high, and is situated on a kind of saddle between two heights. Granite blocks and large fragments lie scattered abroad over the whole of the settlement. The houses lie on a gentle slope, on the southern or south-eastern side of which a small tank is to be seen, that is a collection of water in a natural hollow of the rock. To the north of the place below the slope, on a level spot covered with sandy soil, and overgrown with grass and bushes, lies what I consider to be the burying-place.

The Yemmi Guda cromlechs are all of granite. The solid rock is of such a structure that the uppermost strata may be easily lifted up by a lever. In one instance I discovered a line of little holes made in the rock by a small chisel, just in the same way as the Wāddiwars do at the present day, only that the instrument was much smaller than those now used by them. This was the only trace of instruments I could discover. It is not improbable that these tribes may have used fire for the purpose of raising the necessary granite slabs, and for the erection of them they had certainly some simple mechanical apparatus. Mr. Leonberger told me of a case in which one of his relatives in a village near Stuttgardt, in Wurtemberg, discovered a similar stone grave about ten feet below the surface on a small hill. Mr. Leonberger's description of it corresponds as nearly as possible with your description of those tombs at Jiwarji: the skulls also seem to have been distinguished by the same peculiarities; for the villagers talked for many years of the enormous and curiously-shaped teeth they found in that grave. Beside the skeleton of a full-grown person, there were two *smaller ones* buried in it.

I have forgotten to state two observations, viz., that on the SE. corner of this cromlech settlement the tank naturally formed in the solid granite rock has the appearance of a well, and is from six to eight feet deep. I mention this because it is striking that all the settlements have water near to them, which seems to me in favour of the theory that the large erections above the ground had been used as habitations, and not as tombs, or depositories of urns with human ashes, for which no doubt the lower and half-buried erections were used. The second point which I forgot to state is, that in some parts of the path by which we descended from the hill through the jungle on the southern side towards Mallapur, there were rows of flat stones to be seen laid down in the water-courses, so as to form an ascending path over them up to the settlement. I have no doubt that the occupiers of the settlement laid down these stones, for no other persons could have had any interest to do so in the midst of these jungles. As there is another small settlement down in the valley on the SW. side of Mallapur, it appears that the path between the two places was much frequented, which circumstance would again favour my theory that the large erections on the solid rock were used as habitations, whilst the lower small sandy plain was used as a burying-ground, in which unmistakable tombs are to be seen.

When I was at Guli Guda, talook Badami, I found a cairn and three cromlechs or kistvaens of the smaller size $2\frac{1}{2}$ by 3 feet, half buried in the ground. This settlement is close under a tank, and I have no doubt parts of it may have been covered by the bund. When I was at Dharwar Mr. Young, one of the Assistant Surveyors, told me he found a large settlement near the village of Giwalli, two koss east of Guli Guda. I shall not fail to visit it on my return, and to give you an account of it. (*Extracts from the letters of the Revd. G. Keis*).

REMARKS ON MR. KEIS' OBSERVATIONS.

As far as the Rājan-Kollur and Hegāratgi remains are concerned, I cannot agree with Mr. Keis' hypothesis that the erections were houses. No open cromlechs exist at Hegāratgi; all are closed kistvaens, both at the sides and top, and so closely that it would have been impossible for anything larger than a rat or a lizard to have got inside. Those opened had been deeply let into the earth, and it required a great deal of labour to throw down one of the side-slabs, so as to expose the interior. The contents I have already described as agreeing with those noted by Captain Congreve. All the kistvaens have not the circular aperture; nor where it exists is it in any case large enough for any human being except a mere child to pass through it. None of these, therefore, by any possibility, could have been dwelling-houses of full-grown adults; for we see by the skeletons, that though these people were not tall, yet they were thick-set and stout, and the idea of anything but the largest cromlech containing a family is not tenable.

At Rājan-Kollur there are a few cromlechs open to the south, but by far the greater number of the erections are kistvaens closely put together, and all that I opened, whether with holes in the side, or without, contained the same urns full of charcoal, earth, burnt bones, and ashes, as at Hegaratgi. Many of these are upon the solid rock, and others where the soil is a few inches only in depth ; but in these instances earth had evidently been filled in. What the precise intention or use of the cromlechs was seems to have puzzled many learned antiquaries, and many theories have been advanced on the subject. My own impression is, that they were temples in which the sacred fire was kept burning, and where ceremonies for the dead—perhaps sacrifices—were performed. They have no appearance, beyond their construction, of dwelling-houses, and even the largest of them at Rājan-Kollur,—nearly as large as any yet discovered in the world,—would afford very short and scanty room for a family.

The circles of stones or walls round the cromlechs mark, even more strongly than in the others, their Druidical character. Captain Congreve states that " at Ter Dryn, in Anglesea, are also relics of a circle of stones, *with the cromlech in the middle*, but all are imperfect." And other instances are given of "temples with walls of rough stone about them," not only on the Nilgherris, but in Wales, Anglesea, Dorsetshire, etc.

Of the character of the remains at Yemmi Guda I have no doubt : the only remarkable point about them is that so many should be empty. Closer examination might help, perhaps, to correct this impression as to all, and perhaps also to show that the tombs in the sandy plain below the cromlechs were those of the tribe, or portion of the tribe, which buried the dead ; though, from the fact of there being tops to some cists, this may be doubted ; and that the whole belong to the same tribe at different periods. I much regret that Yemmi Guda is too distant from my district to enable me to pay a visit to this remarkable place, which is evidently worth minuter examination than Mr. Keis had leisure to bestow upon it. The situation of the remains on the summit of a high hill suggests that it may have been one of the fortified camps of these tribes, and it is not improbable that traces of circumvallation or entrenchment might be discovered among the jungles, or on the tops of the hills. Yemmi Guda is situated in H. H. the Nizam's Territory, in the talook of Kanacgiri, and would be easily accessible from Dharwar or Bellary. It is evident to me that many remains not yet known exist in the Dooab between the Krishna and the Tungabhadra; and if the Scythic tribes spread along the Upper Ghats,—which I conjecture to have been the place in the first instance of their irruption,—these remains, and those which exist in the Shorapur country, which I have traced as far as the Bhima, are evidences of the journeys and locations of the tribes to the eastwards, in the direction of the centre of the peninsula where it will be seen they abound.

That the Bellary district has many there can be no doubt, from the subjoined list kindly supplied by Mr. Pelly, Collector of Bellary, who, at my request, collected reports from the Tehseldars of the Collectorate. I expected, as a link between the Southern Dekhan and the Nilgherris, that the Bellary district, and perhaps Mysore, would afford evidences of the residence of Scythic tribes, but I was hardly prepared to find that so many existed as are detailed in Mr. Pelly's list, which amount in all to 2,129. All these lie to the south and south-east of Bellary, and from what Mr. Keis has stated, I am of opinion that others may be found to the NW., and perhaps west also of Bellary. The remains appear to consist principally of cromlechs, kistvaens, and open cists; and it is probable, in regard to the latter, as remarked of the remains at Dhavah-doola-conda, that the top-slabs may have been removed by villagers for their houses. Those at Mudhegāllar, which are the most numerous, are evidently kistvaens, or closed crom-lechs, having four side-slabs, and one as a cover, one of the sides having an aperture in the centre. None, or but few, of these erections appear to have been examined by the Tehseldars, which is to be regretted, though there can be no doubt, agreeing in form and construction as they do with those in Shorapur and elsewhere, that funeral urns would have been found in them. Of the whole, 73 are returned as having walls round them, probably as some at Yemmi Guda, but there is no mention of cairns existing separately from the erections, nor are any measurements recorded. In regard to the whole, there is the same tradition as exists here, in Great Britain, France, etc., that the erections were constructed by dwarfs, and the same name, "Mohorie" or "Mora," agrees with that of these districts. The term "Gujari" is new to me, but appears to have the same local signification as the other.

I was in hopes that some considerable remains might have been discovered in the Dharwar and Belgaum Collectorates; but with the exception of those noted by Mr. Keis at Giwalli, in the Badami talook of Dharwar, I have heard of no others. It is not improbable, however, that direct communications may have been made to Government on the subject by the Collectors, in pursuance of the circular issued.

REMAINS IN THE VICINITY OF HYDERABAD (DEKHAN).

From what I had heard from the late Dr. Walker, whose curiosity and interest had been excited by what he saw of the Druidical remains of this district, I supposed that several groups of cairns were to be met within the vicinity of Hyderabad; but it was not until I had engaged the co-operation of two zealous friends there that I was able to ascertain any particulars of them. They prove to be entirely cairns, and in far larger numbers than I had any conception of, or than exist in the Shorapur country. I have not been able to obtain plans or surveys of the localities as I wished, nor even to have an account of the numbers of the cairns in each, but am enabled by my friends Dr. Bell and Captain Doria, to give some interesting particulars of cairns that have been opened by them, and of their contents.

1st. The cantonment of Secunderabad is six miles north of the city of Hyderabad. At the western extremity of it, beyond the horse artillery lines, and those of a regiment of native infantry which adjoin them, there is a large field of cairns on the slope of a rocky hill, leading down to the Hassain Sagor Tank. These are described to be of single and double circles of stones; the cairns to be placed irregularly as to position—that is, not in lines or rows; and of all sizes, from 12 to 24 feet in diameter; the area enclosed in the circle-stones being heaped up with small stones and earth, forming a small tumulus. There are no cromlechs or kistvaens. I am not aware that any of these have been opened; at least I have no particulars of any.

2nd. Near the hill or rock of Moul Ali, about four or five miles NE. of Secunderabad, and in an open elevated plain, part of which forms the Hyderabad race-course, there is another large field of cairns, containing, I understand, some hundreds similar to those noted above. Some of these have been opened, and I subjoin an account of two received from Dr. Bell:

"We have again been at what————calls the sinful occupation of digging up men's bones, and with some success; as in one or two respects the cairns are different from those at Narkaïlpalli, although not materially so. Hampton and I opened two at Moul Ali, where they are in plenty. The same arrangement of the parallelogram exists, and the same directions are taken as at Narkailpalli—the long direction of the graves (N. and S.); and the peculiarity consists in the tops not being covered by granite slabs. In one it was partially so, but in both, the whole interior was filled up with loose stones and earth, evidently not carelessly thrown in, but placed with care. This made it tedious work for the coolies, and destructive work to the pottery, for scarcely any was got out entire. However, what was recovered does not differ in shape from the drawing of that which you sent me. The *bones are all mixed*, so that I could trace no position likely for a body to be placed in."* In one cairn the articles in the accompanying sketch (No. 9) were found. The bell is very perfect, and is copper, with an iron tongue, which is still *in situ*, and movable. The other things I take to be links of a chain. There are several. The size of the interior of the cairn was nearly the same, 6 feet long, 6 feet 6 inches deep, and 3 feet broad. Both the cairns here and at Narkailpalli are near trap (greenstone ?) dykes, and at both places the circles are formed with blocks of granite, and the central pile, of black stones from the dyke.

3rd. At a small village about midway between Moul Ali and the cantonment of Bolarum there is another group of cairns, similar in all respects to the others, but not so numerous: of these, one or two have been opened, with similar results to those of Moul Ali.

4th. The discovery of these groups led to investigations in other quarters, and Captain Doria, who is employed in the construction and repair of the high-roads to Masulipatam and Madras, found that the high-road at Narkailpalli and Haitipamla passed through large fields of them. Hearing of these, Dr. Bell, in whose division of statistical investigation these villages are situated, visited the spot; and I copy his letter to me on the subject :—

"I have just returned from Narkailpalli, and certainly there are cairns to be seen in abundance : a large patch to the

* This agrees with the confusion observable in the Jiwarji and Andola cairns.

south of the travellers' bungalow, another to the west, and a third to the south of the village, the shape of each being a parallelogram ; but I did not observe that the circles were arranged in diagonal lines or straight ones, and there were no upright stones to mark the regularity of the position, as you described to me. The circles described by the stones were so variable in diameter as to give me the idea that no regular arrangement had been attempted, but the parallelograms extended from east to west in all. The generality of these cairns have immense quantities of small stones thrown upon them ; some a few only, and others none ; and it was one of the latter that I opened. After clearing away the earth to the depth of 2 feet 6 inches, we came upon the covering slabs, which were three in number : these were raised, and the size of the enclosing slabs measured. The side ones were 5 feet 10 inches by 5 feet 4 inches, the end ones 2 feet 4 inches by 5 feet 4 inches, the one at the bottom 5 feet 10 inches by 2 feet 4 inches. The top was closed by three pieces. On clearing away the fallen earth, we came upon a row of pots at both ends, and in the centre a skeleton, lying in such a position as to leave no doubt but that the corpse had been placed upon its belly. A piece of iron was found among the bones of the left hand. In one of the urns were portions of the bones of a child calcined ; the rest were empty, or partially filled with earth.

"This no doubt was a small cairn ; for two others had been opened by natives, and the slabs in them (which they were unable to remove) were double the size I have mentioned, and so also were the diameters of the superficial circles. This was only 16 feet from east to west, and 18 from north to south. In all three the graves extended north and south, and my skeleton had its head to the north."

I enclose a sketch of two of the vessels. (Vide Nos. 4, and 5 of Sketch No. 10). Dr. Bell subsequently informed me that he had met with patches of cairns in the Elgundal Sircar, near the Jaghir village of Telghir, in latitude 18° 35', long. 77° 16, six miles from the large town of Tarapilli: these differ in no respect from those he had seen before, and he regrets he had not time to examine them.

Captain Doria, who was encamped on the same spot, made several excavations at Narkailpalli, and I subjoin his letter on the subject, dated 12th April 1852, Camp at Kātāngur :—

"I received a few days ago your letter relative to the cairns, about which I shall be glad to give you any and every information in my power. I opened ten or twelve of them at Narkailpalli, and other places, but they were so tremendous in size and depth that it is a work of some considerable labour.

"They present themselves in this part of the country in large masses or numbers, never in any regular figure, but generally along and around the base of some stony slope or hill, though they do occur on the open plain and banks of the river. Whether the former positions have been assumed from the facility of procuring the stones which fill up the upper part of the mound which caps them, and of the large circles of stones which encircle them, I know not; but it is an observation I have made, that they are always in a stony vicinity. They are innumerable about here, amounting to thousands: you can hardly move two or three miles in any direction, without meeting some of them. From the Musy river, on both banks, in a SE. direction by Anapilly hill and Narkailpalli, where they surround the hill, (800 feet high on the north side), and extend a little to the east; there are none on the west, and only a few on the south, but some hundreds on the north, some very large. At Haitipamla, and down to Devarconda, they abound. The high road runs through a regular field of them at Haitipamla ; but, with the exception of the stony vicinity, I do not see any peculiarity in their construction or position in regard to one another.

" In size there is a difference, some being of gigantic dimensions, and composed of blocks of stone, very difficult, nay impossible, to remove without mechanical assistance, both as to the size of the stones which compose the outer rings of the tumuli, and also the large slabs which form the inner cell or tomb wherein the body or bones are placed. The diameter of some of the large tumuli is from thirty to forty feet; others again are much smaller, and on them a much less amount of labour has been bestowed. The depth of some of the large ones is very considerable. You first dig through a mound of from three to five feet deep, out-cropping, and bounded by these immense circle-stones, and composed within of smaller stones and earth, which brings you down to the level of the ground about. When you dig down again some eight or ten feet, you reach the regular tomb, which is composed of eight immense slabs of gneiss or granite, forming an enclosure of eight to nine feet long and four to five feet broad, giving a total depth from the top of the mound to the bottom of sixteen to twenty feet. In digging through the mass of earth I have invariably found earthen jars of various shapes, some with covers, some open like saucers, and others much like the earthen chatties now used by natives, except that some are beautifully glazed, and something in shape like these figures, placed at the south corners or feet of the tombs, and about half away between the slab and the top of the ground. These jars sometimes contain calcined bones, but others are merely full of earth, as if they had been placed there empty, or filled with something that has decayed, (I conjecture rice or grain), and given place to native earth.

" In the cell itself, which is always filled with white-ants nests, I have always found more jars similar to the first, and filled, like them, with burnt bones and earth. I have generally found the skeleton entire under white-ant earth, but the bones so decomposed that they have fallen to pieces almost on the slightest touch. The cells are always due north and south, and the skeleton placed in the same direction. At the head, or north end, I have generally found a piece of iron, which might have been a knife or a sword, but almost rusted away, and also arrow-heads of the double-barb shape. In one I found a mass of iron, which must, when new, have weighed several pounds. I also found round the neck of a skeleton a charm or ornament, composed of enamel, and bored through, for suspension I imagine. In some of the cells an upright stoneslab, some two feet high, divides the cell into two parts, always longitudinally, that is north and south. In one cell I found a bell of copper, much corroded, about an eighth of an inch thick, and six inches diameter, which I shall send you with some of the pottery, and shall be glad to open more cairns for you if you wish it.

"I do not think myself that these remains are so ancient as people imagine, but I incline to the opinion that they belong to a wandering race of people, Nomads, whose only habitations, except their tents or huts, were those built for the dead ; for people who could build so well and so substantially for the dead would surely have left something in the way of temples or other buildings for the living contemporary with the tombs, if they had existed as a settled people. The bones found in the pots lead me to suppose, either that only one sex was burned, and the other buried, or that each tomb was not the resting place of one individual, but that each belonged to a family ; and that when a second body was buried, the bones of the first were taken up, placed in a jar, and reburied. In the tombs with a division two bodies were in each, one on either side. I am not enough of an anatomist, nor are the bones so strong as to bear the handling, necessary to determine the sex of the owner." In a subsequent letter he writes: — " I have not been idle about the cairns : we have found several other masses or groups of them : but as yet the ground is so fearfully hard that I have not opened them. There is a village a few coss from this, Nacracul, where the people tell me there is a coss of land covered with them." Again, " Camp near Devarconda " :—" The cairns are innumerable about here, and of immense size ; they are composed inside of one enormous slab below, two sides, two ends, and one or two slabs on the top, built in this fashion with a division about two feet high in the centre, lengthways. The depth of the cairns about ten feet, all north and south, with the skeleton laid north and south, *on its face.* No one seems to care for the cairns, or to open them. The people say they were built by the Rajuses."

Captain Doria again wrote, 13th August, forwarding me the two copper bells, one from Moul Ali, the other from Narkailpalli, and the copper cylinders, arrow and spear-heads, pottery, etc., which I have drawn from actual measurement (sketches numbered and attached) : all these articles will be transmitted to the Society on the first opportunity. Captain D. mentions that he has discovered another new place, where there must be at least two thousand cairns, and is about to open several of them for me. Should I hear anything of interest from him, it shall be transmitted hereafter as a postscript to this communication.

CAIRNS NEAR GURMATKAL.

As I was proceeding by dāk last year to Hyderabad, I observed what appeared to me a large field of cairns about two miles west of this town ; the circle-stones were large blocks of chert. I had not time to examine them closely, and, unfortunately, having been detained, I passed the same place at night on my return, but I have marked the locality for future investigation, as lying nearly midway between Shorapur and Hyderabad, on a high and fertile plateau, which breaks into deep grassy and woody ravines to the south, while the country is amply supplied with water; it would in all probability have been a favourite resort of the nomadic tribes, and would serve to prove that they had marched off to the north-east from Shorapur instead of north or north-west to the Central Dekhan.

It will be evident to the Society that the whole of the Hyderabad cairns are of the same character as those in the Shorapur district, on the Nilgherris, and in Europe. The same circles of stones, some gigantic; the same interior cists, differing only in the quality and size of the slabs used; the same vessels interred, having in them calcined bones, ashes, and charcoal; the skeletons in the cists; the calcined bones of children in urns; the iron implements and weapons, beads, etc.; the same laborious and patient construction of the cists and graves; above all, the discovery of two *bells*, leave no doubt whatever in my mind of the identity of the whole as Scytho-Celtic or Druidic monuments, and completes the only link wanting in the chain of identity. The discovery of a bell has been wanting in the Shorapur cairns as yet opened, but it is evidently a matter of entire chance where one may be found. Captain Congreve mentions that he opened forty-six cairns in the Nilgherris, but only found two bells; Captain Doria ten or twelve, and only one; Dr. Bell three, in one of which one was found. It is probable, perhaps, that these articles were sacred in the families of chiefs or priests, as they are among the Thautawars of the Nilgherris at the present day, and that the cairns in which they are found were those of chiefs or priests. I subjoin a few extracts from Captain Congreve s article, not only to prove the identity of these bells with those in cairns at the Nilgherris, but to substantiate the Celtic-Scythian character of these and other articles.

Mr. Hough, in his Letters on the Nilgherris, says :— "A few of these barrows have been opened ; in one were found *iron heads of spears*,, about four inches long, very well finished, and in a perfect state, but they began to corrode soon after exposure to the air. The same barrow contained *one bell* entire, and the broken fragments of another.

"Hearne, who is justly ranked with Leland, Ashmole, and Anthony-a-Wood, as an eminent antiquary, tells us that on one of the stone monuments at Stanten being opened, it was found to contain a spear, and a large *bell* with a screw at the end of it.

"Douglas, in his *Nenia Britannica,* recording the opening of the barrows in Greenwich Park, states that among other articles found in them were *spear-heads, iron knives* and some cloth.

"The resemblance thus shown to subsist between the Thautawar and Scythian barrows and their contents is too striking to be the result of accident : the fact of so unusual an article of grave furniture as a *bell* being found in both cases is very singular.

"In opening a cairn six miles to the north of Conoor, *two bells* were found among a great number of other antiquities.

"I said lately that bells were frequently found in digging open the cairns ; indeed I discovered two in a cairn at Conoor. With reference to this fact, and in further proof of the cairns having belonged to the ancestors of the Thautawars, I quote the subjoined passage from Harkness' description of a singular aboriginal race, inhabiting the summits of the Nilgherri Hills—

"'A bell, which is generally deposited in some niche within the temple, is the only object to which they pay any reverence. To this they pour out libations of milk, but merely as to a sacred implement. They do not sacrifice or offer incense, or make any oblations to it, significant of its having any latent or mystic properties.

" 'To each Teriri (priest) is attached a herd of milch buffaloes, part of which are sacred, and from which the milk is never drawn, the whole being allowed to go to the calves. One among these sacred animals is the chief. Should it die, its calf, if a female one, succeeds to its office. Should it have no female calf, the bell before mentioned is attached to the neck of one of the other sacred ones, and being allowed to remain so during that day, a legal succession is considered to be effected.

" 'In the morning the Pol-Aul milks one portion of the herd, carries the milk into the temple, leaves the bell with a small portion of it, and of such portion of it as he may not require he makes ghee.'—*Madras Journal,* No. xxxii. pp. 95, 96.

" The bell was an object of superstitious regard among the Celto-Scythians, who buried it in their graves. Speade, in his *Chronicles,* represents an ancient Briton with a lance in his hand, to the end of which was fastened a bell."

The foregoing will, perhaps, be deemed sufficient proof in regard to the Celtic-Scythian character of the bell, as found in the cairns in the Hyderabad country. In other respects, of pottery, burial of the dead, etc., there is, as I have already stated, no difference worthy of notice. The colour of the pottery also agrees with those of the Nilgherris, and these again with those of England. Captain Congreve remarks on this subject :—" It is very remarkable that the resemblance between the urns found in the English barrows and the urns of the Nilgherris extends even to the material. In some of the Dorsetshire barrows the urns are made of a highly finished and glazed red pottery. Many of the Nilgherri urns have been admired for this rich red glazing, particularly one discovered by Mr. Moegling. The zig-zag or arrow-headed moulding, which is the usual ornament of the Celtic urns, is conspicuous on all found on the Nilgherris. I have not as yet found any entire urns with the zig-zag moulding, but I have seen it in several instances on broken pieces of pottery, red and black, found in the cairns."

Need I trace the analogies further? I think not; as in what I have detailed there must be ample proof, to the most sceptical, of the various points of resemblance and identification on all the subjects I have noticed: that the Celtic-Scythian tribes settled more numerously in the direction of Hyderabad, or SE. from it, about Nalgundah and Devarconda, than they did in this, or even the Bellary district, there can be no doubt. Those tracts, and for some distance along the north and south banks of the Krishna river, are, even still, principally low grassy jungle and forest, well supplied with water. They are the favourite resorts of the Brinjaris, who carry grain and salt for the capital, and were no doubt well fitted to the pastoral Scythians. Only a very small portion of that district has been examined by Captain Doria, and it is impossible to say in what numbers the cairns may not exist in other localities of the centre of the peninsula than those he has mentioned. The late Captain Newbold, it is known, had discovered great numbers of ancient remains near Chittoor.

The remains of the Celtic-Scythians as yet discovered in the Dekhan and Carnatic may be classed as follows:

1. Cromlechs without circular enclosures.
2. Ditto with ditto.
3. Kistvaens with and without circular apertures in one monolith, containing urns filled with earth, bones, ashes, and charcoal,
4. Open cists.

5. Barrows containing one or more cairns, as at Shahpur.
6. Cairns with single, double, and treble circles of stones.
7. Cairns with cists of stone below, containing skeletons, remnants of weapons, bells, urns, cups, and other pottery. Shorapur, Moul Ali, Narkailpalli, Devarconda, etc.
8. Cairns containing no cists, but urns filled with ashes, bones, etc., as at Chikānhālli.
9. Temple, or large altar rocks, surrounded by a double ring of large stones and entrance, as at and near Shahpur.
10. Diagonal lines of stones or rocks, as at Vaibāthālli, Shahpur, Ijère, etc.
11. Square platforms, enclosing cairns, as at Māndwalli.
12. The large tumulus and rocks at Shahpur.

The three last have no representatives among the authorities quoted by Captain Congreve, nor among his own discoveries; but who can doubt that they belonged to the same people? The links that are still wanting are—

1. Remains of circular forts, with trenches round them, as on the Nilgherris, Old Sarum, near Stonehenge, and Cærleb in Anglesea.
2. Barrows with trenches round them.
3. Circular basins in beds of rivers.
4. Tolmen, or holes bored in rocks.

Tors and loggan-stones exist in thousands all over the rocky granite hills of the Hyderabad country and Shorapur; and in many places the granite rocks are piled on each other in most fantastic shapes, with separate tors crowning them, and appearing as if a push would throw them over. Many of these may have been sacred.

On all other points, I must consider the identity to be complete, and I am assured that further investigation, wherever these ancient monuments may be found, will only serve the more to confirm what I have already detailed.

I am not sufficiently experienced in the antiquity of this subject to presume to offer more than a few very general observations upon it; but I cannot believe that one of such general antiquarian nd ethnological interest can fail to excite attention and investigation, in proportion as the actual monuments of Celto-Scythic tribes are found to exist in India, and, being examined, are found to agree in all respects with those of Europe. I cannot, with the ample proofs before me, admit the opinion that such resemblances are merely accidental, as is suggested by the Revd. Dr. Schmid in a notice of the subject in connection with the papers of Captain Congreve and the Revd. W. Taylor. In no country that I am aware of are the rites of burial of the ancient inhabitants so marked and peculiar in character, and so entirely agreeing in detail as those of the Celto-Scythic tribes in the east and west; and if the aborigines of India had been all of the same character and religion at the period of these remains, it is only fair to suppose that these cairns and cromlechs would not be found confined to particular localities, but would be universal all over the continent; and their construction, defying alike the hand of time and the changes of faith, would have preserved them wherever they had existed. Further, that had this particular and very peculiar mode of sepulture been universal among the ancient tribes of the world, they would be found to exceed any that have been as yet discovered, whether in Europe, or in Asia and India, and would also be more generally diffused than they are found to be. Many parts of Africa are well known, and have been carefully observed by antiquarians, ancient and modern; yet I am not aware that any trace of Celto-Scythic occupation, as existing in these monuments, has ever been discovered. Though Dr. Carter surmises them to exist in Southern Arabia, which is far from improbable, America, South and North, has its ancient graves and tumuli of a character peculiarly their own. In Europe they are by no means universal, being confined to particular localities, where from authentic history it is indubitable that Celts of the Druidic faith overran the country, and finally settled. In India, it is true, we have no such confirmation by history, and the migrations of the tribes from Scythia cannot be so distinctly traced south-eastwards by these memorials as they can be to the west. The Romans and Greeks have preserved historical records of the migrations of savage pastoral and warlike tribes from Central Asia from time to time, and through many ages, to the west, where they gradually settled, but there are none such in India ; and reverting to those dark ages when India, before the Buddhists and their successors the Hindus, was a country without civilization of any kind, possibly inhabited by a Hæmetic race, we may presume, from the memorials we find to exist corresponding with these general migrations of the Celtic-Scythians, east and west, that other hordes of the same people at a far earlier period of time may have directed their course southwards, and gradually settled in those fertile spots in India where we now find their remains. Mere distance appears to be no objection to this hypothesis ; nor, in the nature of the country, nor its climate from Central Asia to the Dekhan and Southern India, is there any physical obstruction to the gradual migration of hordes of pastoral people, alike from their food and habits accustomed to rapid travel and conquest. After settlements had been made, it is not, perhaps, probable that the original stock of invaders was long reinforced from their native country. Other outlets for emigration were found east or west, and these were followed with greater perseverance, and up to a later period of time, on account of the more temperate and bracing climate to which they led, than those to warmer and more relaxing regions.

By what routes these tribes invaded India I will not presume to assert ; but it is not improbable, I think, if public attention is continued to the subject, and the Provinces of Scinde, Lahore, etc., or those which, from geographical position, afford most presumption of having been the routes of migration, are duly explored, that traces may be found of the same memorials as exists in the Dekhan and Southern India, which would amount to proof, or strong presumption, of the lines of march. In the act of migration, the graves and stone erections would necessarily be more incomplete than those constructed by a settled people ; but it is not, perhaps, improbable, that evidences of settlements would be found.

Assuming, then, from the ancient monuments in existence in the districts I have already enumerated from my own observation, and from those in more Southern India, on the Malabar Coast, (the Pandoo Coolies) and especially on the Nilgherris, (all agreeing generally and particularly in construction and contents, not only with each other but with those of Europe with which we are best acquainted), that Celto-Scythic tribes did inhabit these countries,—we have fortunately, in corroboration, the most interesting proof, perhaps, of all, that they were such, in the roots of their ancient languages being traceable in Tamul, and from it to Canarese, Teloogoo, and Malyalum. Dr. Schmid's knowledge of the present dialect of the Todawars or Thautawars enables him to state that this, with the more modern languages just mentioned, "are links of a closely connected and unbroken chain of dialects of one original language ; and that the Todawar dialect is by far more closely connected with the Tamul than the Canarese." He, in fact, assumes it to be more ancient than the Tamul, which in its turn is more ancient than the others. Captain Congreve gives some striking resemblances of words in use among the Todawars with Celtic, Gothic, and ancient Tamul ; but the most striking and interesting fact

I have met with on this subject is that given by Dr. Schmid, who states that Dr. Ruckert, Professor of Oriental Languages in the University of Berlin, had discovered, and independently from his own studies and investigations, that the Tamul language has a remarkable analogy with Tartar dialects. Dr. Schmid is therefore confirmed in his previous supposition and hypothesis, " that by comparing the genius of the Tamul language with that of other tongues, the race or tribe which afterwards split into Tamulians, Malialis, Canarese, and Telingas, must be a Caucasian or Himalayan race, and must have immigrated into the plains of India very early." Nor, in connection with this, is it the less remarkable, that the memorials which exist should *only to be found* in the districts in which one or other of these dialects of Tamul or Tamul itself, at present exist. That of Shorapur is Canarese. of the Hyderabad Country Teloogoo, of Mysore and Bellary Canarese, of the Malabar Coast Malialum, while pure Tamul exists in Arcot, etc., where these remains are found. I have no doubt, therefore, that under the encouragement for inquiry and identification which presents itself in all forms, these eminent philologists and others will continue their investigations on the subject, which cannot fail to prove of the highest interest, and which, even beyond the fact of actual remains, will establish the migrations and settlements of Celto-Scythic tribes by the roots of their ancient language—the highest proof of all. In the Revd. W. Taylor's paper (No. xxxiii. *Madras Journal of Literature and Science*) I find the following speculations, which have reference to the above, and may be quoted in illustration :

" When the Pauranical accounts of the Hindus close, the ascendancy of barbarous races is mentioned. Sir William Jones gives the names Abhira, Gardabin, Cauca, Yavana, Turashcara, Bhurunda, Maula. Wilford gives Abhiras, Sacas, Tushcaras, Yavanas, Maurundas, Maunas, and Gardhabinas ;

and Southern Tamil MSS. as stated by me in *Or. Hist.* MSS. vol. i, p. 247, give Abiral, Gardhabiyal, Buva, Phigal, Yavunal, Maruntiral, and Mavunal. Now of those names the Abhiras are probably Affghans, the Sacas are Scythians, *i.e.*, Siberians; the Tushcaras, Parthians or Turcomans, and the Marundas or Maunas, or Mavunal, most probably Huns. It is now some eleven years ago since I read a little Tamil book prepared by the Revd. B. Schmid for a seminary, and I found him stating from German authorities that the Huns had ravaged India as well as other countries. I have very recently conversed with Dr. Schmid on the subject; and I believe that there are many German works that may throw light on the emigration of people from east to west. Wilford considers the Marundas or Maunas to be Huns. The Tamul has no aspirate, and Mavunal may be (without the Sandhi) Mā-Unal, the great Hun people. The Abhiras are sometimes considered as equivalent to Ar-viral, or six-fingered people; and tribes so distinguished are said to have been known. A wide field enough is certainly opened; but if the Celtæ were known in Lesser Asia, by the names of Titans and Sacks, and as the Cymri in Wales, that alone is almost sufficient to throw a light upon the existence of cromlechs in the Carnatic. For the Sacks were doubtless a branch of the Sacæ or Scythians (not descended from Gomer, but closely related); then it may follow that the Danes, Cymri and Scythians had customs in common—the use of the cromlech (I will add cairn also) being one of them; and that the Sacæ or Scythians penetrated through the length and breadth of India seems more than probable."

Of the existence of barbarous tribes in India before the establishment of Hindu dominion, there is ample proof, which I need not enter into. We see that under the irruption of Bhuddistic and Hindu tribes, that the aborigines of India, for so these Celtic tribes must have been in relation to them, were gradually absorbed; that their language was changed, and their mode of life; that village communities were established; towns, cave and other temples gradually completed; and civilization, and the use of written language, and with it theology and science, gradually introduced. It must needs have been in the outset that these civilizing influences, carried forward by more powerful and more warlike tribes than the Scythians or their rude descendants, who probably encountered them, soon obliterated in Southern India all traces of the ancient Druidic faith, and that the people who had held it either mingled with the conquerors, or fled into impenetrable jungles, or mountains inaccessible to them. Such a remnant we may well presume the Todawars to be. Their almost European colour, and Caucasian features; their pastoral lives and social customs, food, mode of burial, and sacrifice; their great antiquity, as allowed by the Buddagars, and traceable beyond the Pandawar dynasties—the memorials of whose victories over them are found upon the Druidic cromlechs; the great number of cromlechs, kistvaens, cairns, barrows, circular forts, etc., etc., and their contents, agreeing with those of the plains—probably the most ancient; their even present freedom from idolatory, while surrounded for ages by Hindus; their reverence for the sun and fire; even their mode of dress, all corresponding with Celtic customs and usages; above all their language, admit, I think, of no doubt that they are the only true remnant in India of the most ancient of the Scythian tribes, and that they were driven to the Nilgherris from the plains, where I believe these memorials to be more ancient than those on the Nilgherris, and more purely Scytho-Druidic. Captain Congreve classes the remains on the Nilgherris into three kinds. The oldest are the simplest. In the others are found traces (by figures, etc.) of Buddhistic or Jain corruption which occurred probably when the Jains had possession of the hills, and from which the Todawars are again become free. The height of the mountains; the coldness of the climate;

the deep belt of almost impenetrable jungle, which surrounded them on all sides, and its extreme insalubrity—all combined to preserve them from any serious molestation by the Jain or Hindu kings; and the salubrity of the climate above, suited to their originally hardy constitutions, has preserved them hitherto in vigour, though reduced to a comparatively small remnant.

I will not attempt to offer an opinion on the antiquity of these remains. Druidism, or Druidic-Scythism, one of the most ancient religious beliefs of the world, is here evident; and while we find that all comparatively modern irruptions of Central Asiatic barbarians into Europe, the Huns, the Getæ or Goths, the Alani, etc., were idolaters, we are carried back insensibly beyond them to the ages of a simple faith which was held by their progenitors, and followed in those parts of Asia and Europe in which the emigrant hordes gradually settled, where their memorials are found to exist. The identity of these remains, however widely separated from each other, I can see no reasonable ground to doubt under the evidences before me, and trust that the Society may be enabled to obtain such further information of Scythic monuments, and their contents, as may lead to a more complete understanding of the districts inhabited by the tribes. My impression, however, is, that they will be found principally in, if not entirely confined to, the central, southern, and western portions of the peninsula—in short, to those districts in which the traces of their ancient language are most apparent.

"But what the same historian, Herodotus, liv. c. 71, 72, relates concerning the ceremonies observed at the funerals of their kings is still more extraordinary. I shall only mention such of those ceremonies as may serve to give us an idea of the cruel barbarity of this people. When their king died, they embalmed his body, and wrapped it up in wax: this done, they put it into an open chariot, and carried it from city to city, exposing it to the view of all the people under his dominion. When this circuit was finished, they laid the body down in the place appointed for the burial of it; and there they made a large grave, in which they interred the king, and *with him one of his wives,* his chief cup-bearer, his great chamberlain, his master of the horse, his chancellor, his secretary of state, who were all put to death for the purpose. To these they added several horses, *a great number of drinking vessels,* and a certain part of all the furniture belonging to their deceased monarch, after which they filled up the grave, and covered it with earth."—Rollin's *Ancient History,* vol. ii, p. 467.

Extracts from Mr. J. Babington's *"Description of the Pandoo Coolies in Malabar," (Trans. Lit. Soc., Bombay, vol. iii, p. 324.)*

Like the Pandoo Coolies on the eastern side of the Ghauts, the Kodey-Kulls, Topie Kulls, or Pandoo Koolies, are generally to be found on the tops of eminences, or on the sloping sides of such hills in Malabar as are not wooded. They seem to vary in their shape according to the nature of the soil or rock on which they are constructed." The Kodey Kull consists of a stone like a native umbrella (from which it takes its name) placed over an excavation, and the Topie Kull an erection shaped like a mushroom: in the former, urns, human bones, arms, iron instruments of various shapes, and sometimes beads of different shapes, colors, and materials, were found, but in the latter nothing. "There are many places in Malabar where the Kodey Kulls are found; but in no situation do they exist in greater numbers and preservation than on a hill named Chataperambah, which is excavated in every direction with caves of this descriptions. It is singular that the Malayalum or Malabar name of this place should give a complete description of it; being literally *the field* (compound, etc.) *of death,* Chatum peramba. Whether this coincidence is accidental, or the name was given to it originally, and handed down to the present race, I know not; but I am inclined to be of the latter opinion, as there are several other places in the district with the same name, and I understand also of the same description with this spot, which is situated on a hill rising abruptly from the southern bank of the Beypoor river, and about five miles to the eastward of the village of that name." "It is almost unnecessary to say that there is no record of these antiquities, of the period of their construction, or the use for which they were originally intended."

Statement showing the particulars of Dwellings of Human Beings

(Communicated by C.

No.	Names of Talooks	Names of Villages	Distance and direction from Bellary		No. of Dwellings	Particulars of			
			Direction	Distance, Miles		Having a slab of stone on each of three sides as walls, and one above as roof, leaving one side open.	Having a slab of stone on each of four sides as walls, and one at top as roof, one of the side-slabs having an aperture in the centre	Having a slab of stone on each of four sides as walls, and one at top as roof.	Compounds or enclosures built of stones enclosing dwellings of the above three descriptions
1	Koodilghee ..	Halsargaum ..	S.	45	200	..	..	..	..
2	Hoovinhudgully	Rajahvalum ..	S.	56	33	..	..	..	31
3	Raidroog ..	Mullapoorum	S.	30	485	..	3	..	18
4	,, ..	Addagoopah	S.	30	525	..	..	..	17
5	,, ..	Gollahully ..	S.	30	200	..	..	..	6
6	Kodecondah ..	Kondapoorum	SE.	..	1	..	..	..	1
7	,, ..	Poolair ..	SE.	..	1	..	..	..	..
8	Dhurumaveram	Moodheguloor	SE.	..	580	..	580	..	..
9	,, ..	Dhavadhoola-condah ..	SE.	..	104	104	..	..	..
		Total			2,129	104	583	..	73

N.*B.*—Four of the sketches and the figures of the Bells, Pottery, &c., which accompanied Captain postponed for a future *of diminutive stature, situated in the Bellary District.*

PELLY, ESQ., Madras C.S.)

Dwellings			
Having a slab of stone on each of four sides as walls, without any at top.	Having a slab of stone on each of three sides as walls, without any on the fourth side or top	Having a slab of stone on each of four sides as walls, without any at top, one of the sides having an aperture	Extracts of Urzees of Tehseldars on the subject
200	..	..	Tradition says that former Governments caused dwellings of the descriptions alluded to to be erected for a species of human beings called Mohories, whose dwarfish stature is said not to have exceeded a span when standing, and a fist high when in a sitting posture, who were endowed with strength sufficient to roll-off large stones with the touch of their thumbs. The dwellings in question contain nothing.
..	2	..	It is said that these dwellings belonged to a sect of human beings called Mohories. It is not known when and by whom they were erected for the Mohories, nor is any description given of them.
48	132	284	It is said that human beings of a diminutive size, called Mohories, occupied these dwellings.
51	243	214	It is said that these dwellings belonged to Gujaris, by whom they were anciently inhabited.
85	81	28	It is said that these dwellings belonged to Gujaris, and, that they were anciently occupied by that class of creatures.
..	..	..	It is said to be a pagoda of the Pandawahs. On being dug up, a smooth long stone was found therein.
..	..		It is said to be a pagoda of the Pandawahs. On being dug up, some iron nails and plates were found therein.
..	..	..	It is said that human beings, dwarfs, called Gujaris, resided in these dwellings ; that they were erected with no other material but flags of stone, from fear of showers of fire, and that the beings were under a yard in stature. One or two of these buildings were dug up, but nothing was found. The dwellings situated near Dhavadhoolacondah are without the flags that were placed on the top as roofs ; they were carried away by the merchants of the village for their houses. It appears that a being of the description above given from Podhatoor visited Culliandroog a short time ago.
..	..	..	[No measurements of any of these remains have been forwarded.—M.T.]
384	458	527	

Meadows Taylor's paper, have been lithographed, the rest, with the plans, are unavodiably opportunity.—*Secretary.*

Reprinted from the Transactions of the Royal Irish Academy,
Vol. XXIV, Part III, Antiquities, pp. 329-362

ARTICLE V

DESCRIPTION OF CAIRNS, CROMLECHS, KISTVAENS, AND OTHER CELTIC, DRUIDICAL, OR SCYTHIAN MONUMENTS IN THE DEKHAN

By Capt. Meadows Taylor

With sixty-four Illustrations from his Original Sketches and Surveys

Read May 12, 1862

In the year 1850, my attention was first attracted to these ancient remains, by observing the large group of cromlechs near the village of Rajunkolloor, in the principality of Shorapoor (an independent native state, situated between the Bheema and Krishna Rivers, immediately above their junction), of which I was then Political Superintendent. They were called by the people, in the Canarese language, " Mori-Munni," or "Mories'" houses; and these Mories were believed to have been a *dwarf race* of great strength, who inhabited the country in very remote ages. There were two groups, separate, and situated about half a mile from the village westward, in some rocky uncultivated land which sloped gently to the south ; and, strange as the fact of Druidical, Celtic, Scythian, or Aryan remains existing there appeared to be at first, subsequent investigation proved beyond a doubt that these, and others which will be detailed in this paper, were indeed such.

I regret that I cannot submit plans of both of these groups of remains; but that of the smaller one, Plan No. 1 (Plate

IV), will explain the positions of the cromlechs in relation to each other, and also of cairns or barrows which exist in connexion with them. The larger group consists of, perhaps, one hundred cairns and cromlechs, small and large, and occupies about five acres of ground. The scale of the plan (Plate IV) will give the dimensions of the smaller one.

In order to ascertain the nature of these remains, and their contents, I had several opened—large and small, closed and otherwise. The interior of the closed cists contained a little black mould on the surface, a few inches thick; below this, the earth was greyish white, known to the people of the Dekhan as "Pandre Mutti," a substance which has an antiseptic quality, and had evidently been brought from another locality, as it did not exist on the spot. With this earth, human ashes and portions of bones and charcoal were mixed; and pieces of broken pottery, red and black, also appeared. These remains rested upon the solid rock, upon which the cists had been constructed.

No entire urns, or spear or arrow heads, or other remains, were found in any of these kistvaens or cromlechs; nor was there any difference in the contents of any of them. Grey earth, mixed with portions of bones, human ashes run into a rough slag with sand, and small pieces of charcoal, were in all; and the inference was, that the ashes of burnt human bodies had been placed there, and perhaps originally in urns; but why they should all have been found broken was not intelligible, as there was no appearance of disturbance of the monuments.

Many of the closed kistvaens had round holes in the centre of the slab on the south side. The diameters of these holes varied; but were never more than 9, or less than 4 inches. What the particular use of these perforations was, is, I believe, a disputed point among antiquarians; but it is at least remarkable that this peculiarity is found to exist in similar remains in Brittany, in England (Kitts Coty House, near Boxley, in Kent, being, I believe, a well-known example), and in Circassia, according to Mr. Bell ; and, with the descriptions of such monuments, those at Rajunkolloor entirely agreed.

I here make a distinction, whether correctly or not I cannot say, between kistvaens and cromlechs. They are similarly constructed, except that the former—whether with or without a top—has always four sides, and the latter only three. In none of the open cromlechs could anything be found, and the original earth of the floor remained undisturbed. Indeed, in most instances, they were placed on the solid rock, or where

SKETCH No. I.

the surface soil was very shallow.

The size of these monuments differed very widely; the smallest being oblong, about 10 inches wide, and 2 feet long, probably graves of infants; the larger having interiors 8 to 10 feet long, by 6 to 8 feet broad.

I beg to submit herewith an original Sketch No. I, made on the spot, of a portion of the largest group of kistvaens and cromlechs; and I found the dimensions of the slabs of which the large cromlechs are composed to be as follows:—Side pieces, 15′ 3″ long by 9′ 0″ broad, and 1′ 9″ to 1′ thick. The top covering slab is 15′ 9″ long by 10′ 9″ broad, and 1′ to 2′ 9″ thick; the interior space being 8′ by 6½′, open to the south

Another, somewhat smaller, in the foreground of Sketch No. II, has a top slab 12 feet by 10 feet 6 inches, and 9 inches to

Sketch No. II.

1 foot thick, and the side slabs 12 feet 2 inches long by 8 feet broad. In a third the side slabs are 9 feet high, 12 feet 3 inches long, and about 1 foot thick. In this kistvaen, the slab containing the round hole is to the south. The sketch also gives a view of part of the general group, including those of which ground plans are given.

Comparing these monuments with the dimensions of the cromlechs near Newydd in Anglesea, they do not appear much inferior in size. The great one there, which I believe is one of the largest known, has a covering stone 12 feet 7 inches long, 12 feet broad, and 4 feet thick; another, near it, is a square of 5½ feet only.

The slabs of stone, of which the largest monuments at Rajunkolloor are constructed, were obtained from a very peculiar formation which exists about three miles to the west. Here granite in a state of fusion, has disturbed the stratified limestone and sandstone, and to some extent vitrified both, and the latter-named material, though much more difficult to quarry, was preferred to the stratified limestone, which could have been obtained close by. It is difficult, however, to conceive how those large slabs of stone were quarried—for the rock is very hard—or transported to their present locality.

Plan No. 2 (Plate V) is of another remarkable group of cromlechs and kistvaens, connected with cairns, near the village of Hegāratgi, about four miles west of Rajunkolloor. There are twenty-three cists here, and twenty cairns, two of which are of large size. The whole are irregularly disposed on a piece of waste land, also sloping to the south upon the left bank of the River Dône. Those marked with crosses were examined, generally with the same result as at Rajunkolloor in regard to contents. But one cairn contained urns of red pottery, which were full of ashes and partially calcined bones. All these monuments were constructed of limestone slabs, and rested upon the solid granite rock as foundation. The limestone lies naturally in laminæ, which are from 1 inch to 1 and 2 feet in thickness; it is, therefore, easily quarried, and can be broken by a hammer, or even a hard stone, into flags of any size. No surface dressing, therefore, was required, and the sides and top stones of these kistvaens were smooth, and at once available for use, after having been shaped to the size required.

Plan D, annexed (Plate VI), gives the ground plan of the largest kistvaen in Hegāratgi. The dimensions of the side slabs are 15′ 6″ long; the cross pieces being 6′ each. In the front slab was a round hole, $5\frac{1}{2}$″ in diameter; the top was 11′ 3″ long by 7′ 4″ broad; so that it projected a little beyond the upright sides. The sides fitted very neatly; but, whether from damp or other causes, none of the urns inside were whole, and what were found crumbled away on exposure to the air. There were two upright stones on each side of the entrance slab, which I did not remark in any other cist.

In another kistvaen were found seven large pots, or urns, the dimensions of one being 3′ 9″ high, and 2′ 3″ in diameter; but none of them could be removed whole. They contained ashes, charcoal and fragments of bones.

Plan No. 3 (Plate VII-A) is also of a group of cists and cromlechs, with cairns, at Belsettee Hill, six miles north-east of Rajunkolloor which needs no particular explanation, the remains being of the same character, though not so perfect or so large.

The foregoing localities were the only ones in the Shorapoor district where, to my knowledge, cromlechs and kistvaens above ground exist; but on the hill of Yemmee Gooda (the Hill of the Buffaloes), about seventy miles to the south of Rajunkolloor, in the Raichore district, there is a very large and remarkable group (*vide* Plan No. 4, Plate VII-B). These remains occupy a tolerably level spot, near the top of the hill which has once been rudely fortified. Here are sixty-five cromlechs and kistvaens, many of large size; and, as a new feature, four of the largest are surrounded by double circles of large stones. Thus also, at Ter Dryn, in Anglesea, the cromlech is surrounded by a circle of stones. The whole lie among the immense granite rocks of the locality, as shown in the plan; and on the west side of the cromlechs are a number of graves, formed by slabs of granite let into the ground, with cross pieces at the head and feet; forming, as it were, sunken cists. The dimensions of the largest cromlech here are: side slabs, 9′ long by 6′ 5″ broad; top cover, 7′ broad by 9′ long, and 1 to 2 feet thick, many others being nearly of the same dimensions.

I now pass to the subject of cairns, which, in relation to their construction, the remains found in them, and their complete identification with similar monuments in Europe and Central Asia, afford, if possible, more curious and more strictly corroborative results than the cromlechs and kistvaens. I shall first notice those at Jiwarji, the largest and perhaps the most complete group in the Shorapoor district, and beg reference to Plan No. 5, Plate IX. The Sketch No. 3 (Pl. VIII) also shows the appearance of a portion of this cemetery, as taken from the north end.

Jiwarji is situated about three miles south of the Bheema River, on the high road from Shorapoor to Gulberga, and the cairns are found beside the high road, about two miles south of the river, on a piece of waste, sterile ground which slopes gently to the south, and is composed of yellowish-grey argillaceous shale, with a covering in some parts of shallow black earth from 3 to 6 inches thick; in others, the earth has been entirely washed away.

I would here beg to remark, that all the groups of cairns, cromlechs, or kistvaens, which I have found in the Dekhan, have been placed upon ground which slopes gently to the south.

In this respect I have observed no variation anywhere. Also that all cairns in which urns were to be deposited, or cists of stone to hold bodies, were dug in dry shale, gravel, or hard earth; and that the surface of the ground was unculturable land. The space enclosed or occupied by this field of cairns measured 336 by 216 yards; and there were 268 cairns counted, with many others difficult to decide upon. The number of stones in the circles is 24 to 36 in the single ones, and 48 to 68 in the double. Some of the cairns had open cists at the top, composed of flags of limestone, which projected a foot or more beyond the surface. The stones placed round the cairns are black trap boulders, some of large size, which were brought from the trap hills to the west. These black circles, therefore, resting here upon light-coloured yellow and grey argillaceous shale, have a striking appearance, and could not be mistaken. In all of them, the spaces contained within the circles have been filled with earth and stones till a small tumulus was formed, rising to the centre.

The Cairn A, in the Plan, was first opened by a trench run through the barrow on the top, 4 feet wide, and was commenced between two slabs of limestone which had been placed on the south side, near two of the circle stones. These slabs, which were upright in the ground, were 2 feet apart, and lay N.E. and S.W. by compass. In all the cairns also, afterwards examined, precisely the same result ensued; and the direction of the cist below the ground invariably corresponded with that of the entrance stones above. Carrying on the trench, loose stones and earth were found, and removed to a depth of 5 feet in the centre. Below this, the ground was very hard; and, to all appearance, the natural shale had not been disturbed. Nothing was found in the trench; and for a time, further examination was given up.

The Cairns B, C, D, and E were next tried, with similar results, and I began to suppose that whatever had been interred had perished long ago. But observing in A two-trap boulders on the southside, below the excavation already made, and sloping downwards—which could not *naturally* have existed —further examination was continued, and it was curious that those boulders corresponded with the direction of the limestone slabs in Cairn C, and formed an entrance, as it were, to the body of the grave from the S.W. side.

About 5 feet below the level where the first excavation had terminated, a cist formed of neat limestone slabs was found; in which, among some white earth, the bones of a skeleton were distinctly traced, and the skull recovered, though not in a perfect state. This skeleton lay on its face, and below it were two smaller ones, of which the skull of one was remarkably thick. These skeletons lay N.E. and S.W. by compass, as indeed all afterwards found also did. A red cornelian bead of oblong form, pierced, was the only article found in the cists; but when the earth behind the near slab was examined, some small vases or urns of red and black pottery, a few decayed spear and arrow heads of iron, and an iron tripod, were found. The largest skeleton measured 5 to 5½ feet in length from the top of the skull to the toe bones; the others were 4′ 11″ and 4′ 9½″, respectively. I may here remark that all the skeletons found in these and other cairns were of small size as to height, but having bones of unusual strength and thickness. It is certain, also, that the tradition of the constructors of these monuments being dwarfs—a tradition which, I believe, prevails wherever these remains are found—should correspond with what was found, indicating at least, people of low stature.

Cairns B, C, and D yielded much the same results; and I show figures of a small sickle and bill-hook found in Cairn B.

In Cairn B, however, the discoveries were so peculiar, that I beg leave to detail them separately.

Two regular and complete cists, formed of limestone slabs, were found at the bottom of the grave, 12 feet from the surface. That on the east side contained one skeleton, which

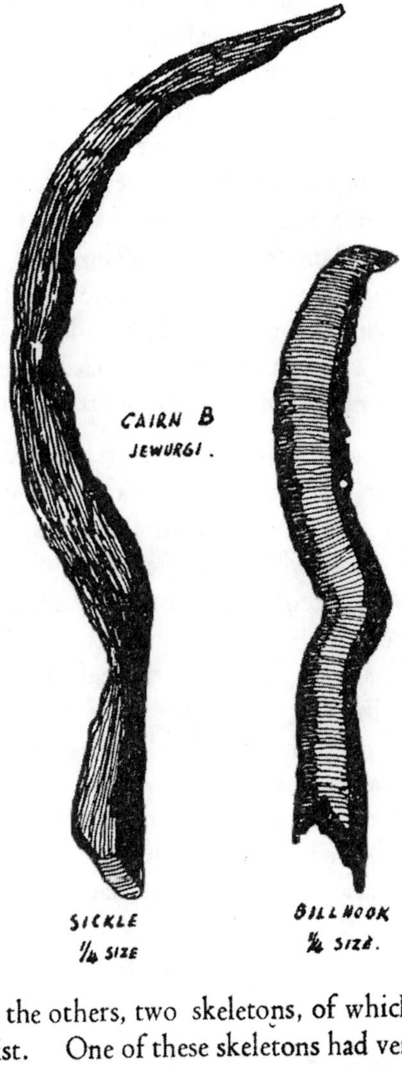

was perfect; the others, two skeletons, of which one skull *only* was in the cist. One of these skeletons had vertebræ attached to the spine, above the clavicles, but no skull; and there was no reason to suppose, when all else was distinctly seen, that it had decayed. These skeletons were indeed so perfect, as they lay in the dry earth, which had been carefully picked away, that every particular could be observed. Now, the skeleton which had a skull, had been laid down on the left side, and the face should have corresponded to this position, but it was found turned quite the contrary way—in fact, towards the back of the skeleton. The inference at once was, that this corpse had been beheaded, as well as the other, and the head placed as it was found. These skeletons appeared to be those of women ; and the bones of the pelvis were very broad and strong. Amongst the earth above the cist, remains of several other bodies were found ; but none of the skeletons had been laid down regularly ; they had evidently been pitched in at random, and were in all sorts of inclinations and positions ; nor was there any one skull found near or attached to a skeleton.

Cairn D—the exterior of which corresponded as nearly as possible with that of Cairn C, except that the diameter was larger—was next examined very carefully. After the crust below the loose stones which appeared to be the natural shale of the excavation, beaten down till it had become concrete—had been removed, the same greyish earth as in other places (*Pandre Mutti*) was met with ; and gradually portions of skeletons, lying literally in all directions among this earth. How many there may have been could not be ascertained, but five skulls were taken out tolerably entire, though they soon crumbled away on exposure to the dry hot wind ; and there were pieces of others, and also of children's skulls observable. A section of the excavation is given in Plate X.

About 9 feet from the surface the lid of a cist was met with, and the excavations carried on on the N. W., S. W., and S.E. sides, till the cist was completely laid bare. It consisted of limestone slabs, varying from 2 to 4 inches in thickness, which may have been quarried from the bed of the small river which runs past Jiwarji, and bounds the south side of the cairn field.

Five slabs, 4′ 6″ to 4′ 8″ long, were laid down as a floor (*vide* Fig. I, Cairn E). Upon these, three slabs, lengthwise, and 6½ feet long, were set as uprights ; and four slabs, 20 inches and 1 foot, respectively, apart, were placed between at head and foot to form two divisions, 18 or 20 inches wide on the east and 1 foot on the west. In the division on the west were small urns, many of them broken ; but some were got out whole, together with two arrow heads, a sickle, an iron tripod, a cornelian bead with a hole drilled through it, and what may have been a sword, broken into two portions and much decayed.

CAIRN D

IRON TRIPOD

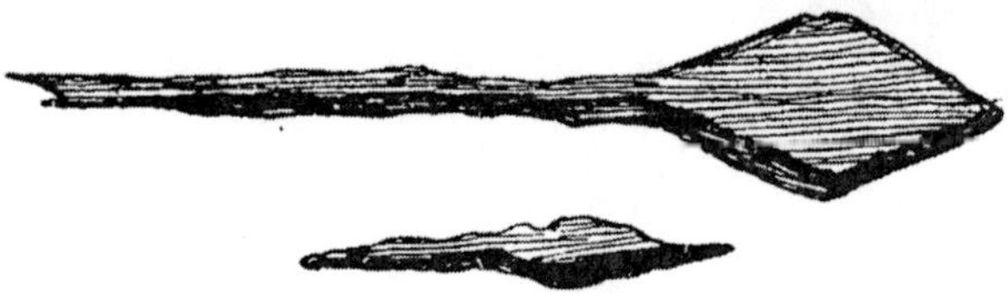

ARROW HEADS

The division to the east contained two skeletons, laid on each other, both *face downwards*, the skulls of which were in their proper places ; but, curious to observe as it indeed was, one skull was met with in the centre of the bodies placed upright, with the face to the earth, which belonged to another skeleton—for the two in the cist were, as they lay, singularly perfect, male and female, the male below ; nor could the skull have fallen from above, for the covers of the cist corresponding with the floor were quite entire.

At the head of the cist, in the space between the cist and the shale of the excavation, a great number of small vessels of pottery had been placed, the earth about which was removed very carefully. Now, in doing this, another single and separate skull was met with, which had been placed upright on a ledge, as it were, of the shale, looking to the foot of the grave, and just above the pots. It was so perfect when taken out that I hoped to preserve it ; but having been incautiously placed in the sun, it crumbled away almost to powder in a few hours. This skull could not possibly have belonged to any entire body placed in the cist, for it was separated by several feet from all others, and its position, as also that of the extra skull in the cist, was too remarkable to be mistaken. A tracing of part of it, when first taken out, is given below.

Here then, appeared unmistakable traces, and proofs indeed, of human sacrifice ; and another cairn, E, was then opened,

CAIRN D

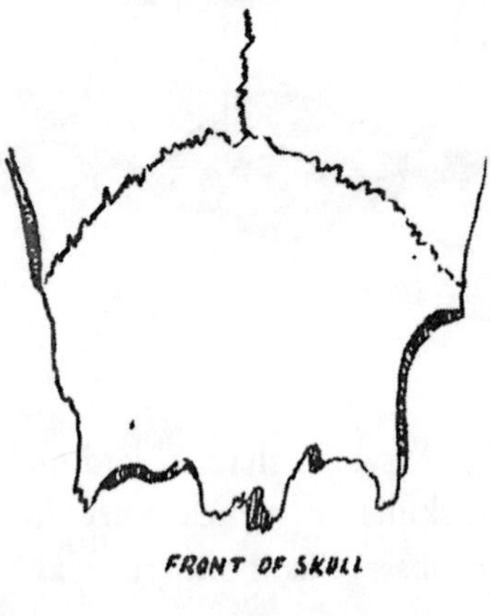

FRONT OF SKULL

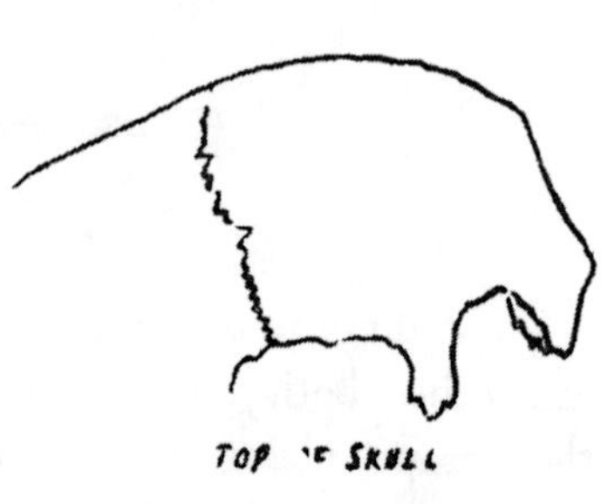

TOP OF SKULL

(Plate XI) and if possible, more carefully examined. As the excavation proceeded downwards, remains of six skeletons in the most irregular positions conceivable, were found, and skulls, of which three were tolerably perfect, and were separate from the bodies. I had directed the excavation to be carried down first to the foot of the cist, should there be one ; and at the usual depth of 9 feet a cist was found, very perfect, the covering slabs of which were removed as the work proceeded ; and the earth about the cist which remained was carefully picked out, so as to leave nothing unexamined. Near the head of the cist, and resting upon some earth above the end covering slab, some bones were met with, and, on the earth above them being carefully picked away, a perfect skeleton was shown in profile, without a head, and with the skull placed in the centre of the body, with the face to the south. It had really so ghastly an aspect, that it took some persuasion to get the workmen into the grave to go on with the work.

This skull proved to be very perfect, and the bone had not changed into lime, so that I was enabled to make a tracing of it, which I now show below.

Cairn E

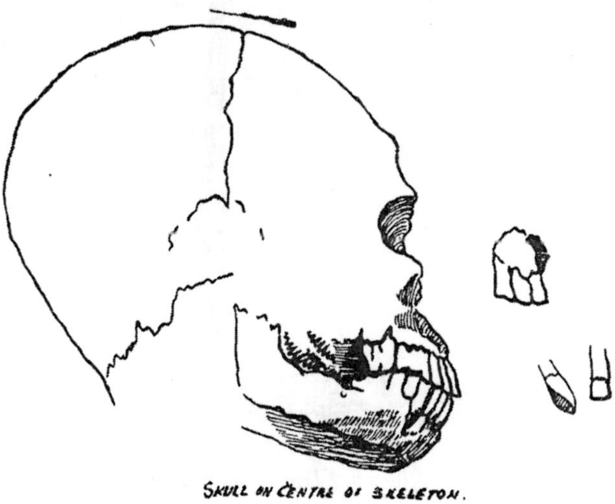

SKULL ON CENTRE OF SKELETON.

The cist was 4′ 10″ long inside by 3′ 4″ broad, including the dividing slab, leaving one to the east 2 feet, the other 1 foot broad. In the eastern division were two skeletons, both shorter than the cist, the *upper* with *the face downwards*, the lower one on its left side. In the division to the west was one skeleton, that of a woman, as my apothecary declared, which appeared perfect as it lay ; but no portions of these skeletons could be preserved, owing to their crumbling directly they were exposed to the air. The iron lamp, of which there is a representation, see below : was found hooked into the shale at the head or north end of the grave. The earth on

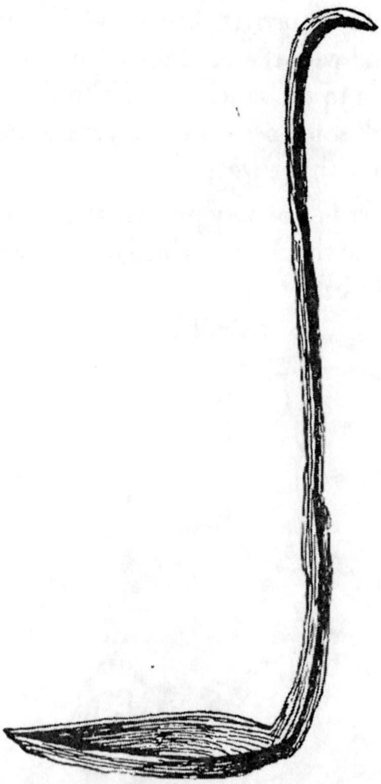

Cairn E, Jiwarji. Iron Lamp, ½ size.

which the remains were found, and which filled the cists, was "*Pandre Mutti,*" of the same quality found in the cists of Rajunkolloor.

These discoveries, which were afterwards confirmed by examination of cairns at Andôla, Narkailpullee, Hyderabad, and other places, seemed to me conclusive as to the establishment of the fact of human sacrifices, else why the number of separate skulls found in such curious positions? Also that the grave had been the burial-place of one chief person, with whom the others were put to death. It would have been as easy to dig a new grave, as to open one of these large chambers, nay, easier; nor could I see, indeed, how a cist could have been opened to put in a new body without removing the whole of the upper earth and stones, and replacing them. I regret I have none of the skulls, or portions of them, to present to the Museum of the Academy. Several were, however, sent to the Museum of the Royal Asiatic Society at Bombay. They were all remarkable for the great thickness of the cranium, and large size of the teeth, of which, in many instances the bright enamel was still perfect.

Plan No. 6 (Plate XII), is of another field of cairns on the lands of Andôla, five miles S.E. of Jiwarji, which consists of forty cairns and cists, irregularly disposed, of which two, A and B, were opened. They were not so deep as those at Jiwarji, owing to the hardness of the shale; but they contained the same description of cists. In both, skulls were found separate from the bodies, and so remarkably, that the native workmen were struck with it. They noted, as they called them, the proofs of murder; and a sort of *procés verbal* was drawn up by the Putwari, or village scribe, who was superintending the workmen. From Cairn A eight very perfect skulls were taken out, and the number of portions of skeletons in all sorts of positions was very remarkable. In short, it appeared just as if, while the white earth was being shovelled into the grave, that the bodies above the cist had been thrown in with it.

In Cairn E the cist was similar to that in A, but in the eastern division was one skeleton only. Strange to say, the skull of this was separated from the body, and lay with its face to the *north*, resting upon the shoulder and left arm, the jaw projecting beyond it, and the top of the cranium being just over the breast-bone—an impossible position for the head, had it not been separately placed there.

I do not think there is further necessity for multiplying examples, though my notes contain many others. The positions of skeletons without skulls lying in all directions; of skulls without skeletons; the very remarkable instance in the Jiwarji cairns of a skull being found, inside a perfect cist, placed upright between two skeletons; and of a skeleton being found lying transversely across the cover of a cist, without a skull, which had been placed upon its middle—all served to impress me with the conviction that the bodies so found were those of human victims; but whether of men or women, I could not determine.

The vases or pots found in these cairns, and also at Jiwarji, (examples of which are given in Plate XIII) had been placed, some at the the head of the bodies behind the cists, others upon shelves left in the shale. They were red and black earthenware, covered with a rough vitreous glaze. One in Cairn A contained some delicate white bones, which proved to be those of an iguana; and another iron tripod was found, which is also figured in Plate XIII. Some skulls and bones of dogs were also found amongst the human remains, but no remains of horses or cattle. Do not these discoveries go far to confirm the description of Herodotus, quoted by Rollin, of Scythian funeral ceremonies and sacrifices?

"After the body has been transported through various provinces, it is placed on a couch, set round by spears; his concubines are then sacrificed, and a mound of earth is raised over the king and his women."

And again—" They then interred the king with one of his wives ; his chamberlain, his master of the horse, chancellor, and secretary, were all put to death ; as also several horses ; a number of drinking vessels were also buried." And these urns, many of which were of small size, may have been drinking vessels.

The deeds of violence of which these graves and their strange remains were witnesses, after so many centuries, probably not less than 3,000 years, perhaps indeed more, agreed, to my perception, with the exception of the sacrifice of horses, with the traditional funereal rites of Scythian tribes—probably Aryan.

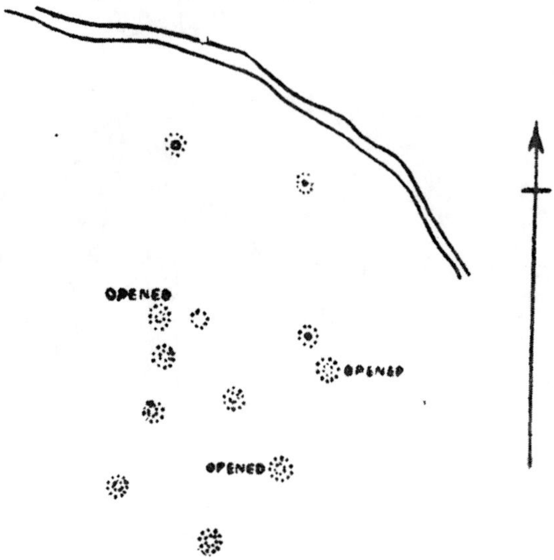

PLAN No. 7

Cairns at Chickunhulli, Shorapoor.

But other divisions of the same people had evidently other rites ; and the examination of cairns at Chickunhulli, eight miles S.W. of Shorapoor, which, to all outward appearance, were identical with those of Jiwarji and Andôla, resulted in the discovery of large urns, containing partly burned bones, ashes, and charcoal, which had been buried underneath. There were no cists in these cairns. The largest of those urns was 3′ 9″ high, and 2′ 3″ in diameter, but it was impossible to get it out whole. Several smaller ones, in excellent preservation, were sent to the Bombay Museum.

CHICKUNHULLI CAIRNS. LARGE URNS, CONTAINING HUMAN ASHES AND CHARCOAL

Afterwards, near Shahpoor, about 13 miles north of Shorapoor, I found an extraordinary parallelogram laid out with rocks (Plan No. 8, with Sections A, B, and C, D), which may possibly have been the place of cremation for the whole district, (Plate XIV). The space enclosed is 400 feet by 260. The natural ground slopes slightly to the south from the north side; and a tumulus had been formed by raising the earth on three sides to a centre, around which, in a diameter of 60 feet, large greenstone boulders had been regularly placed, and a great number irregularly, all over the sides of the tumulus. Outside these were rows of granite rocks, 6 deep on the east, 2 deep north and south, and 2 on the west ; but this part is evidently incomplete, and six rows were apparently intended. Some of the rocks which form the outer boundary are very large, and I give a few dimensions :—

	Long	High	Girth	
1st	10′ 5″	6′ 7″	36′ 9″	At 200 lbs. the cubic foot.
2nd	10′ 1″	6′ 2″	27′ 3″	About 190 tons weight.
3rd	9′ 5″	8′ 9″	23 0″	About 200 tons weight.
4th	9′ 5″	5′ 8″	27′ 2″	

There are 56 of these rocks, varying from the above dimensions, to 6′ long, and $5\frac{1}{2}$′ broad, 3′ 9″ high, 6′ 2″ in girth, which is the smallest of any, or about 4 tons weight. Sketches Nos. 12 and 13, (Plate XV) which were taken on the spot, give the appearance of the east and south sides. These rocks, which are granite, were evidently brought from the Shahpoor hills, a distance of three miles. There is no granite nearer the geological formation changing to gneiss and laminar limestone nearly from the foot of those hills, and there are two deep nullas or rivulets, with scarped banks between, which must have proved a great obstacle in rolling these masses, which is the only means by which I can conceive that they were moved.

Two trenches, 6 feet wide, were carried through the tumulus at right angles, sections A, B, C, D (*vide* Plan No.. 8, Plate XIV), down to the natural floor, which had not been disturbed. The sides of these trenches, which were 8 feet deep in the centre, disclosed layers of human ashes, partly burned bones, charcoal, potsherds and white earth; and it appeared to me that the tumulus had been raised by successive cremations (for it is impossible to suppose that the whole had been raised on one occasion), because of the layers of ashes which, by the sand having run into coarse slag, and the white earth laid over all, separated as it were, each cremation from the one beneath; and that, as each cremation was completed, the place seemed to have been covered with white earth.

The Shahpoor hills, affording pasture and water, were probably a favourite place of resort of these tribes; for the monumental remains about them are very numerous. Of these, Plans Nos. 9-12 (Plates XV and XVI) show some of the most remarkable groups; and that in No. 9 is especially curious and interesting. It is situated close to the village of Vibathullie; and a field has been covered with rocks, generally about the size of the smallest of those of the large parallelogram at Shahpoor, disposed in diagonal lines, so as to leave square spaces between each four—enough in fact, to hold a cairn. The south and west sides have 22 large rocks each, the square of which would be 484 feet, but the north-east corner is not complete. The area was perhaps intended to be an exact square, but actually measures 360 by 340'. Five cairns, surrounded by simple circles of smaller rocks, have been constructed within the lines, of which two are double size, that is, enclosing double spaces. At a little distance to the north-west, twenty-eight cairns, some of large dimensions, are situated near each other, and irregularly disposed.

Plan No. 11 shows another space laid out for cairns by rows of rocks. This is near the east gate of the town of Shahpoor, about two miles north of Vibathullie, and is less complete than the other.

The next plan, No. 12, is of a group of five cairns near Vibathullie, on the way to Sugger, below the Tank (Plate XVII). In this Plan, one large barrow, A, has a triple circle of stones, the outside circle being large rocks about the size of those at Vibathullie, or the smallest of those of the great parallelogram at Shahpoor. This barrow was so hard that it resisted all attempts to break through the concrete of the upper part of it, and I was obliged to leave it unexplored.

An instance of a discovery of a Druidical temple also occurred near the road through the valley leading from the town of Shahpoor to Sugger. It stands amongst the fields by itself, and consists of one large flat-topped granite rock, 22 feet high, with a circumference of 82 feet, and is surrounded by two circles of small rocks, the first 18 feet from the base of the rock, the other 4 feet beyond it. On the south side are two larger rocks placed as an entrance, as it were, on the line of circle stones.

Another instance of rock temple that I have met with in the Deccan, was near the town of Toljapoor, 120 miles north of Shahpoor. This also has a double circle of stones, and near it are several groups of cairns, of which a few were opened, but nothing beyond broken urns and pieces of bone and charcoal were found. They were, however, in all respects, of the same character as other cairns in the Shorapoor district.

Two curious pieces of natural rock, selected apparently for worship by this ancient people, from amongst the countless tors and loggan stones with which the Shorapoor hills abound are given above. Of these No. I is not, perhaps, unlike the Cheese Wring rocks, near Liskeard, in Cornwall, figured in Mr. Godfrey Higgins' book, both being granite of probably the same character. No. II is more peculiar in form, the upper and upright stone resting in a bed on that underneath, and poised as it were on the exact centre of gravity. No. I is 82 feet, No. II 66 feet in height, and belong to the groups of

No. I.

ıidical Rocks, Shorapoor Hills.

No. II.

Druidical Rocks, Shorapoor Hill:

denuded rocks incidental to the district. Both groups, being surrounded by circles of large stones, were, no doubt, used as temples or places of sacrifice. No. I which has two large rocks placed to the S.W. as an entrance to the circle, is still used by the shepherds as a place of sacrifice—red powder and offerings of flowers and milk, being made to the *genius loci* in a natural recess formed by two rocks at the base, overlapping part of the larger one.

Plan 13 shows another area near the village of Ijeyri, laid out with rocks, and two cairns in their allotted spaces.

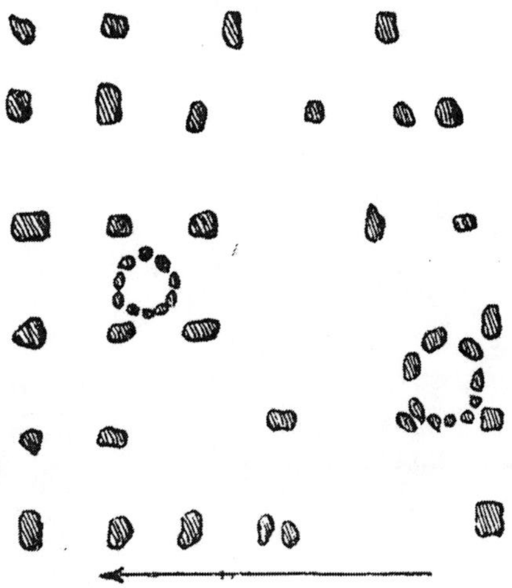

PLAN NO. 13.

Plan No. 14 contains a variety in the construction of cairns, which occurs near the village of Mundewallee about 35 miles N.W. of Shorapoor. The circles of rocks—here boulders of basaltic trap—are triple; surrounded by diagonals of large basalt boulders and smaller stones, packed closely together. The sides of these diagonals are 180 '156', and 126' respectively, the largest being partially incomplete, and, in connexion with the size of the cairns, present a very remarkable appearance. I was not able to examine them: the labour of removing the stones would have been very great.

All the foregoing plans and descriptions relate to remains in the district of Shorapoor only. Many others exist there, but I trust I have given sufficient detail to show the different variations of construction of these monuments, and of the separate uses to which they were applied in that province.

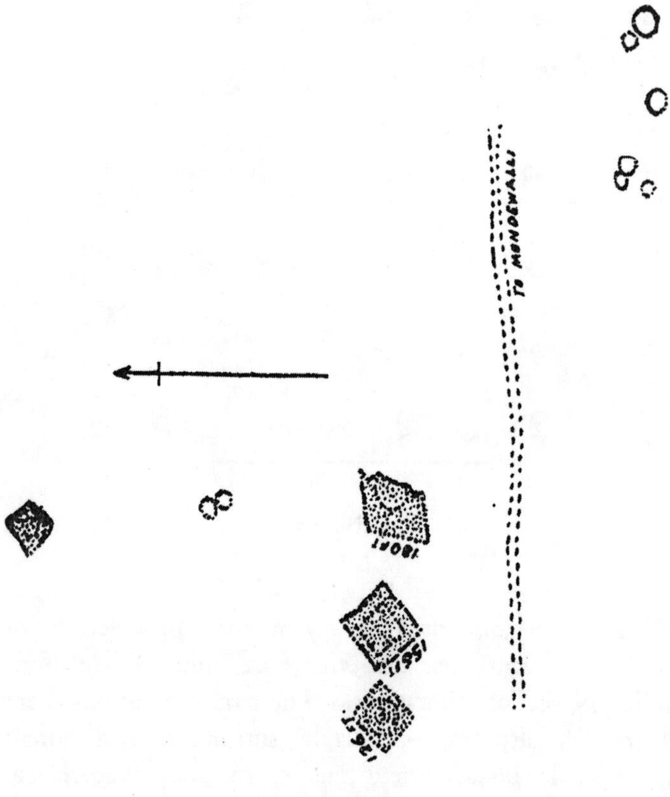

PLAN No. 14

Cairns near Mundewallee, Shorapoor. Scale 160 yards=1 inch.

Having communicated my discoveries to several friends, and requested an examination of some fields of cairns near the city of Hyderabad in the Dekhan, which to all outward appearance were of the same character as those of Shorapoor a few were opened, and results, much the same in character observed. In some, cists were found underground, containing skeletons, some of them lying on their faces ; others, as at Jiwarji, confusedly above the cists. In one cairn a bell, with a tongue attached to it (Fig. 1, Plate XVIII) was found—it had been cast, and was of good finish, the metal being still resonant—with a good many small urns, red and black—some iron links of a chain, spear and arrow heads much decayed, and another bell of wrought copper (Fig. 2, Plate XVIII).

On the road from Hyderabad to Masulipatam, near the village of Haitepamla, there are some large fields of cairns. Again, near Narkailpullee, wrote my correspondent :—" They are literally in thousands, in groups two and three miles asunder."

Several cairns in one of these groups were opened ; and here again results similar to those in the Jiwarji cairns, indicative of human sacrifices, were obtained in the bodies interred in

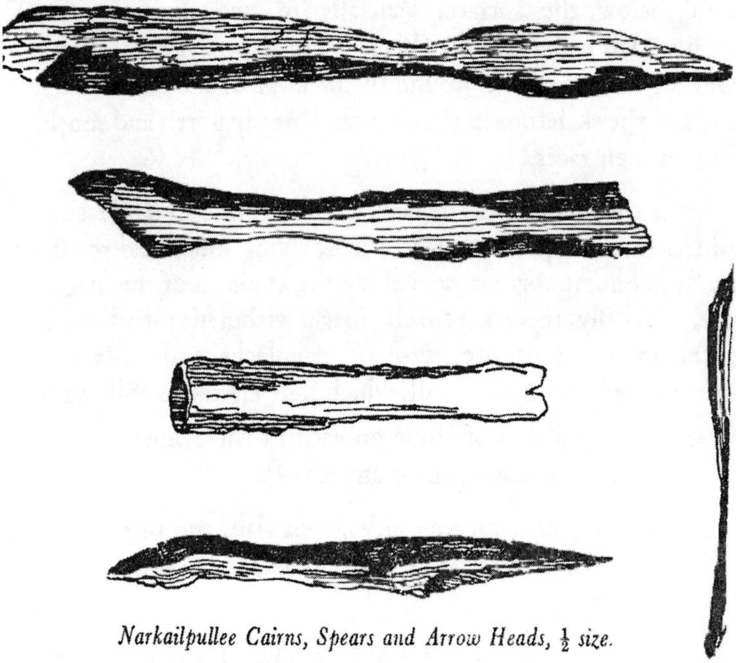

Narkailpullee Cairns, Spears and Arrow Heads, ½ size.

cists below the surface being on their bellies, and in the great confusion of skeletons and bones at top above the cists.

In two instances, here also, bells were found, which form another peculiarly corroborative link between the remains in India and in Europe. Three of those found were sent by me to the Museum of the Asiatic Society of Bombay, where they now are. Of these the most perfect is shown in Plate XVIII as Fig 3. It is of wrought copper, and was evidently used as a cattle neck-bell. Some of the iron articles found in these cairns are also shown (Plate XVIII).

Near the town of Devarconda, in the province of Golconda, S.E. from Hyderabad, a large field of cairns was discovered by a friend employed upon topographical duty. Several were opened, and cists composed of irregular granite slabs were found below the surface, generally in two divisions, the dividing slab being two feet high. The depth of these graves from the surface of the ground to the floor of the cist was ten feet, and the skeletons in the cists lay "nearly north and south, all upon their faces."

From the district of Bellary, a collectorate of large size, perhaps 10,000 square miles in extent, lying south and south-east from Shorapoor, I obtained, by the kindness of the magistrate, Mr. Pelly, reports from all villages within his jurisdiction, of the existence or otherwise of cromlechs and kistvaens. There proved to be 2,129 in all, which were classed as follows :-

1. Having a slab of stone on each of three sides, and one side open (cromlechs ?).	104
2. Having slabs on four sides, roof slab, and one side slab perforated by a circular hole (kistvaens ?).	583
3. Of the above, surrounded by circles of stones.	73

4. With slabs of stone on three sides, open at top. 458

5. With slabs of stone on four sides, open at top. 384

6. With four sides, no top, and one side pierced with circular aperture. 527

Cairns were not reported upon, but I have no doubt they would have been found in great numbers.

Two other very extensive districts were under my charge in succession from 1853 to 1858, each upwards of 8,000 square miles in area ; but in neither Daraseo nor Berar could I find any of these remains, except the rock temple and a few cairns already mentioned near Toljapoor in Daraseo. I have heard that many have been found by the officers of the revenue survey in the Belgaum and Dharwar collectorates, but I believe them to be most numerous south of a line drawn between Belgaum, on the west, and Vizigapatam, on the eastern coast of the Peninsula.

My own investigations and discoveries in Dhorapoor and elsewhere may be classed as follows :—

1st. Cromlechs, or open monuments, with and without circles of stones containing no remains.

2nd. Kistvaens, with and without circular perforations in a side slab and with and without covering slabs, containing human ashes, bones and broken pottery.

3rd. Cairns and Barrows, with single, double and treble circles of rocks and stones, containing cists and skeletons, with traces of human sacrifice, pottery, arms, etc.; others, with cinerary urns interred in them without cists.

4th. Rock temples, with circles of stones round them. as near Shahpoor, Toljapoor and Shorapoor.

5th. Lines of rocks, placed to mark boundaries for cairns.

6th. Square and diagonal platforms of rocks inclosing cairns.

7th. The great parallelogram and place of cremation at Shahpoor.

These, I believe, embrace all forms of Druidical or Scythian remains known, except barrows with trenches round them, circular forts, and dolmen or holes bored in rocks.

It will be evident, also, from the foregoing details, that the ancient people to whom these remains belong were divided into two sects : one of which buried their dead, with attendant sacrifices, in cairns ; the other burned their dead, without sacrifices, and interred their ashes, collected in urns, in kistvaens and cairns. Which of them may have been the elder family— or whether they were co-existent—who can say ?

If this subject, as regards Celto-Druidic or Scythian remains in India, be interesting to the Academy, I would beg to bring to notice a very valuable and interesting paper by Captain Congreve, of the Madras Artillery, which appeared in the "*Madras Journal of Literature and Science*," No. 32 of 18 in regard to his discoveries of Scytho-Druidical remains in the Nilgherry mountains. These consist of large barrows and cairns, with some kistvaens and cromlechs, but none of the latter have the dimensions of those found at Rajunkolloor and Yemmee Gooda. Captain Congreve advances an hypothesis, that the Todurs, the apparently aboriginal tribe which was found exercising signorial rights over those beautiful mountains, and whose existence was not known until a comparatively late period, are the descendants of Aryans or Scythians, who once overran India ; and he goes far to establish this, by the present similarity of their funeral rites and forms of graves with those of ancient Scythian tribes. It may indeed be so, and that their entirely isolated position preserved this remnant from absorption into the people of the country. Their fair ruddy complexion, and their language, do not appear to belong to India.

Two other papers will be found equally interesting in reference to another character of these remains, locally called Pandoo-coolies—one by the Rev. W. Taylor, in No. 33 of the "*Madras Journal of Literature,*" and the other by Mr. J. Babington on the Kodee, or Topee Kulls of Malabar, in Vol. III of the "*Literary Transactions of Bombay.*" I observe that Mr. Higgins gives engravings of those monuments in his work without knowing what they are. The appellation "Topee or Kodee Kull" is derived from their appearance—Topee in Hindee, as Kodee in Canarese, being a cap or covering, and Kull in the latter language, a stone, "covered stones"—being literally what they are.

What I have advanced as evidence of the existence of human sacrifice in Indo-Scythian tribes, and that these Dekhan cairns belonged to Scythian tribes, may possibly receive corroboration in this country by the examination of cairns and barrows for this purpose. If my memory serves me correctly, I have read in a Bath newspaper, possibly of 1858, in the proceedings of the Archæological Society, which held one of its annual meetings there, a paper describing the opening of a cairn or barrow in which similar evidences of human sacrifice were obtained ; and it is very possible that there may be much other European data existing on this part of the subject with which I am unacquainted. I may mention also incidentally that last autumn, when shooting upon a moor in Northumberland, I came upon a group of cairns among the heather, exactly similar to what I had seen in the Shorapoor district. A large cairn of loose stones on the highest part of the moor had been once examined, and remains of weapons, pottery, and the like, found; but the cairns seen by me had never been noticed, though a high, single stone, not unlike that at Rudstone, in Yorkshire, and called locally the "lang stane," is famous in the neighbourhood, and its vicinity had been repeatedly examined by local antiquarians, by whom these cairns were overlooked.

I will not detain the time of this meeting longer, by tracing similarities between the remains I now bring to notice and those detailed in Mr. Godfrey Higgins' work on the "Celtic Druids, and others of similar character, though, for many reasons, I am strongly tempted to do so. It is impossible, however, to compare the views and diagrams given by Mr. Higgins in his beautiful work with those which I now show, without the conviction that, however widely separated, geographically speaking, they must have had their origin in the same people or people professing the same faith, and using the same rites of sepulture. Any one of the cromlechs or kistvaens shown by me might be Kitts Coty House in Kent; while the great army of stones of Carnac, in Brittany, the Druidical temple at Rowldrich in Oxfordshire, or that of Avebury in Wiltshire, have their analogy with the rocks of Vibathullie, or those around the great tumulus of cremations at Shahpoor. The largest rock of Carnac, as given by Mr. Higgins, measures 22 high, 12 broad, and 6' thick, exclusive of what is concealed by the sand, and the weight as estimated by him is 256,800 lbs. The dimensions I give, if none so high, are greater in girth, and on the same data for calculation of weight, 200 lbs. per cubic foot of granite, would be 465,800 lbs., 432,000, and 324,000 lbs. respectively. In relation to the fields of cairns, also, the plan of Stonehenge, with the cairns irregularly disposed about it, agrees with the great group at

Jiwarji, where they are only more numerous ; while the great fields of Narkailpullee, Dewarkonda, Haitepamela, and Goormutcal would, if surveyed and planned, cast the fields of Mr. Higgins' diagrams and my own altogether into the shade.*

Again, the very traditions agree most strangely. Mr. Higgins, page 37, quotes Camden in regard to the stones of the temple at Rowldrich, that "they were believed to be men turned into stones ; they were the king and his soldiers." So, of the rocks of Shahpoor, those round the parallelogram are believed to be men—the largest being the chief—watching black and grey cattle (the black, greenstone ; the grey, granite boulders), lying in the midst. The people of the country, especially the Beydurs, who are no doubt descendants of aborigines, not of Aryans, believe this perfectly ; and also tell you, in regard to the rocks placed at Vibathullie, that "they were men who, as they stood, marking out the places for the elephants of the king of the dwarfs, were turned into stone by him, because they would not keep quiet.

About these "dwarfs" Mr. Higgins gives a translation of M. de Cambry's work, "*Monuments Celtiques*," in regard to Carnac, "that the rocks were an army turned into stone, or the work of the Croins—men or demons, two or three feet high—who carried these rocks in their hands, and placed them there ?" Who can doubt the similarity between these and the "Mories" of Rajunkolloor, Yemmee Gooda, and the Bellary district—dwarfs who built cromlechs and kistvaens, and, as is believed, lived in them, and were buried in the cairns of Jiwarji and other places?

We have proof in the remains figured, that this ancient people were acquainted with the arts of pottery, and of working iron, copper, and bronze ; and in the shape of the sickles, arrow

* NOTE :—The plans of Celtic or Druidic remains on Dartmoor, given by Sir Gardiner Wilkinson in the numbers of the "*Archæological Journal*" of March and June 1862, appear also to tally with those given in this paper.

and spear heads, I find the closest analogy between the remains of the province of Shorapoor, in the Dekhan, and those I see in the Museum of the Academy which have been discovered in Ireland. Of gold or silver I have found no trace ; nor of any article—ear-ring, ring, or brooch—which could have been used for personal adornment.

On all these grounds, I submit respectfully for the consideration of the Academy, that the remains I have now detailed, with those on the Nilgherries and the Topee Kulls of Malabar and Canara, in all their varieties, agree in establishing the identity of the great Aryan Nomadic tribes of the East Celts or Scythians being Druids, with those of the West ; and to show, as I have already remarked, that however widely divergent their wanderings have been, they may be traced by their monuments of worship and sepulture, the almost perfect similarity of which is too remarkable to be doubted.

ILLUSTRATIONS

PLATE I

FIG. 1.
CROMLECH AT AGHENNY NILGH.S

FIG. 2.
KITT'S COTY "HOUSE KENT.

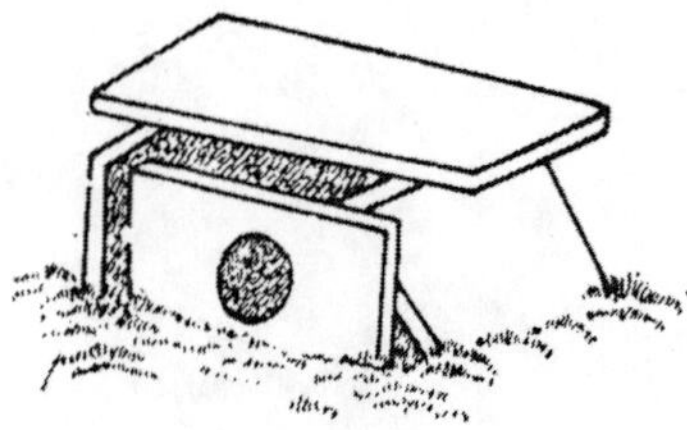

FIG. 3.
FRONT VIEW.

FIG. 4.
SIDE VIEW.

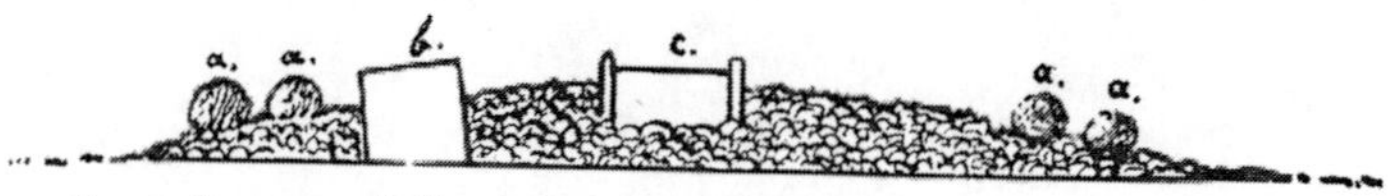

a. a. CIRCLE STONES b. SIDE c. KISTVAEN.

FIG. 5

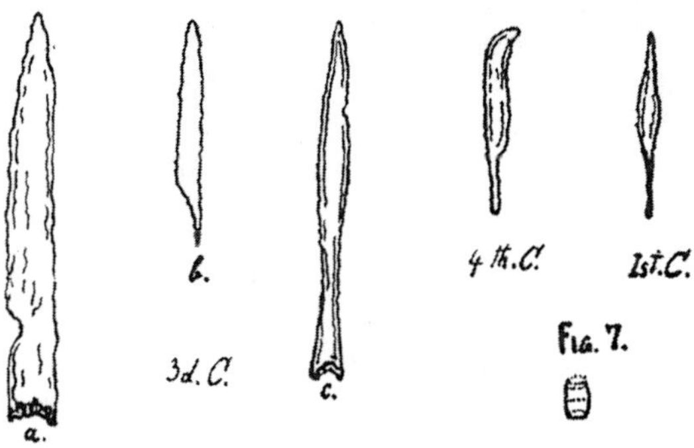

FIG. 7.

MD. AHMAD.

PLATE II

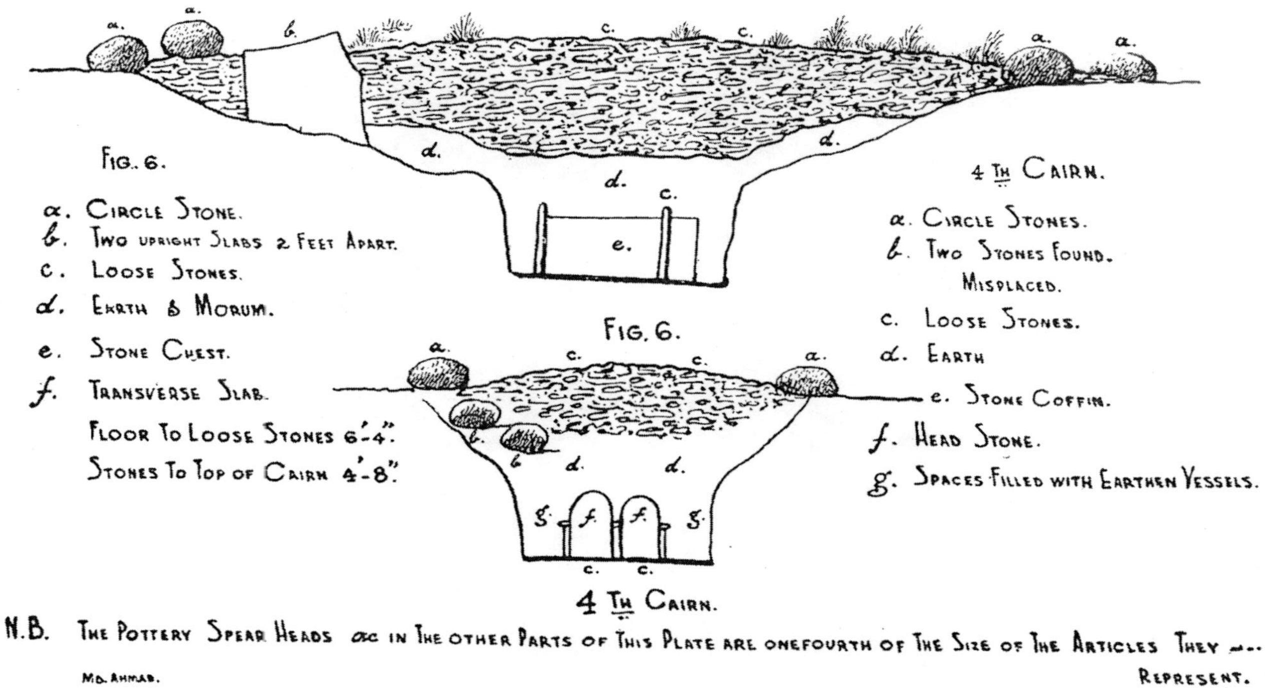

Fig. 6.
a. Circle Stone.
b. Two upright Slabs 2 Feet Apart.
c. Loose Stones.
d. Earth & Morum.
e. Stone Chest.
f. Transverse Slab.
Floor To Loose Stones 6'-4".
Stones To Top of Cairn 4'-8".
4 Th Cairn.
a. Circle Stones.
b. Two Stones Found. Misplaced.
c. Loose Stones.
d. Earth
e. Stone Coffin.
f. Head Stone.
g. Spaces Filled with Earthen Vessels.
Fig. 6.
4 Th Cairn.
N.B. The Pottery Spear Heads &c in The other Parts of This Plate are onefourth of The Size of The Articles They Represent.
Md. Ahmad.

PLATE III

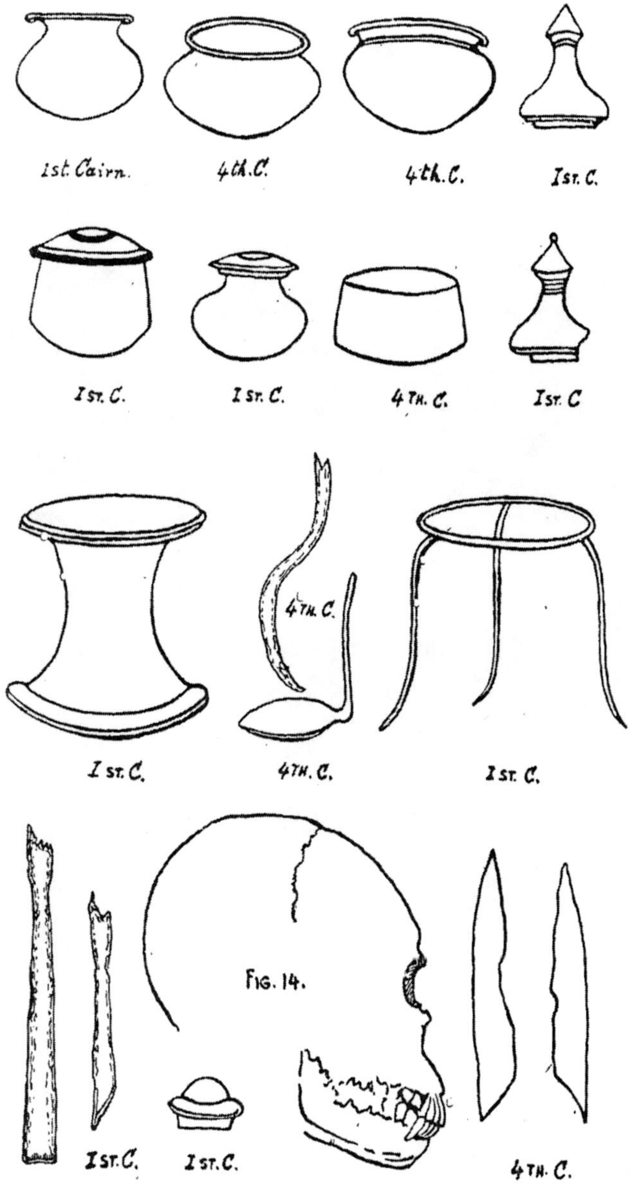

1st. Cairn.
4th. C.
4th. C.
1st. C.
1st. C.
1st. C.
4th. C.
1st. C
1st. C.
4th. C.
4th. C.
1st. C.
Fig. 14.
1st. C.
1st. C.
4th. C.
Md Ahmad.

PLATE IV

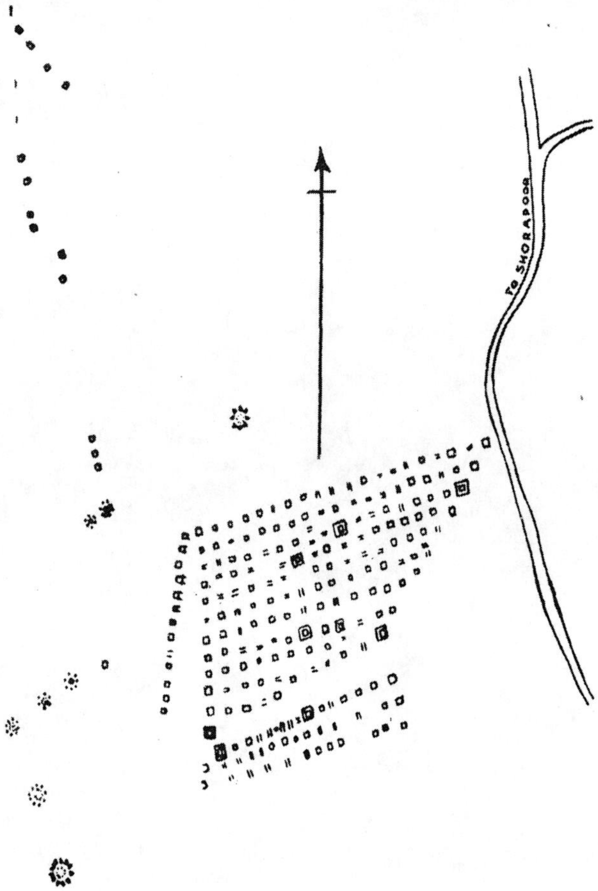

PLAN No. I

Cromlechs, Kistvaens, and Cairns, Rajan Kollur. Scale 160 yds.—1 inch.

PLATE V

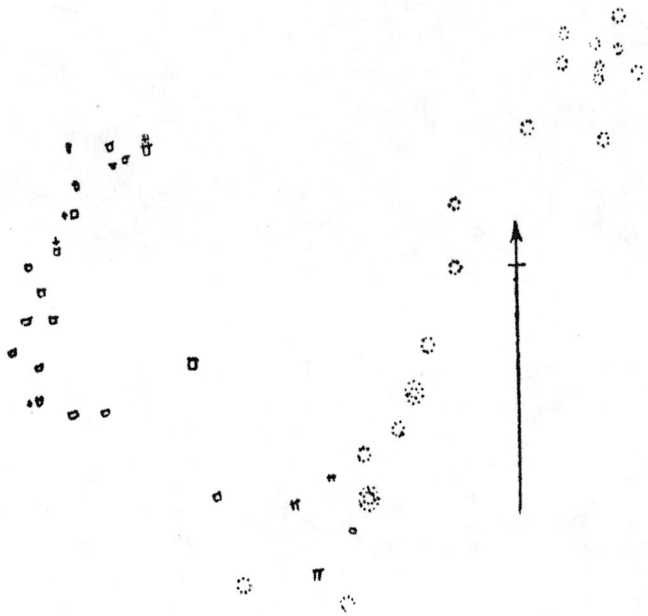

PLAN No. II

Cairns and cromlechs, Hegaratgi, Shorapoor. Scale 160 feet=1 inch.

PLATE VI

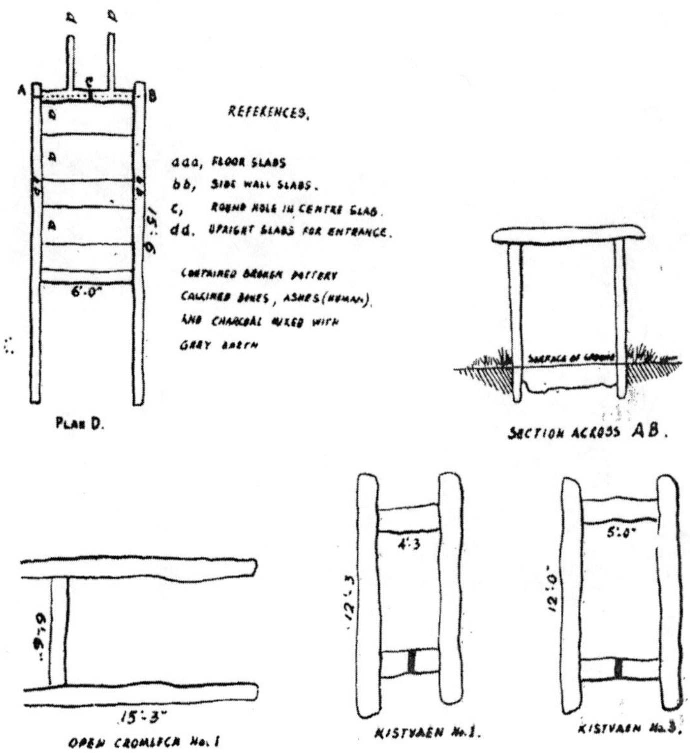

A
B
C
15' 6"
6' 0"
PLAN D.
REFERENCES.
aaa, FLOOR SLABS
bb, SIDE WALL SLABS.
c, ROUND HOLE IN CENTRE SLAB.
dd. UPRIGHT SLABS FOR ENTRANCE.
CONTAINED BROKEN POTTERY
CALCINED BONES, ASHES (HUMAN).
AND CHARCOAL MIXED WITH
GREY EARTH
SURFACE OF GROUND
SECTION ACROSS AB.
6' 6"
15' 3"
OPEN CROMLECH No. 1
4' 3
12' 3
KISTVAEN No. 1.
5' 0"
12' 0"
KISTVAEN No. 3.

PLATE VII

A

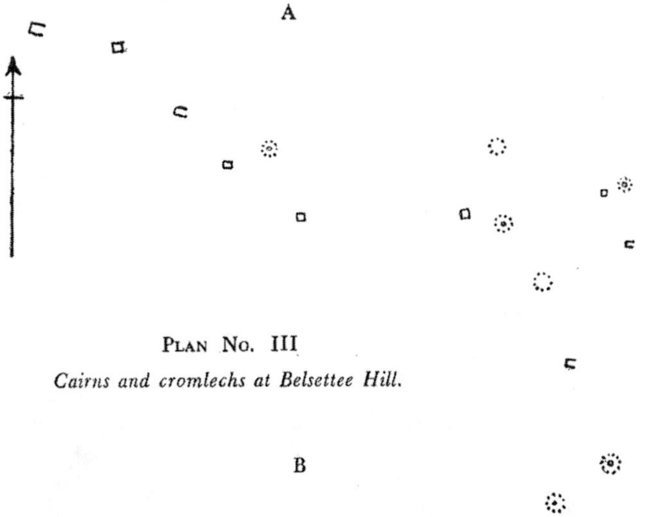

PLAN No. III

Cairns and cromlechs at Belsettee Hill.

B

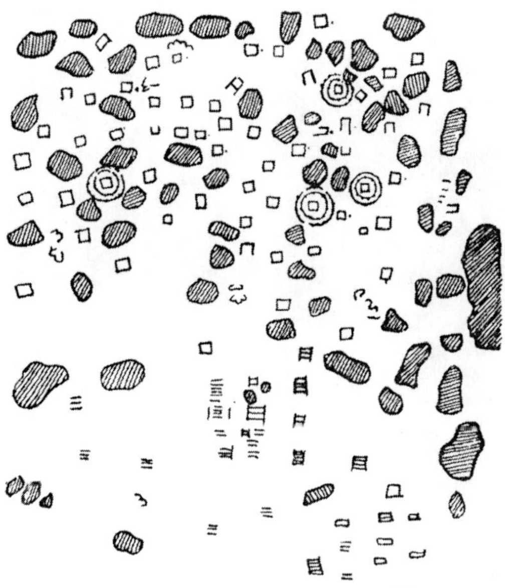

PLAN No. IV

Cromlechs at Yemmı Gooda, Hill of the Buffaloes.

PLATE VIII

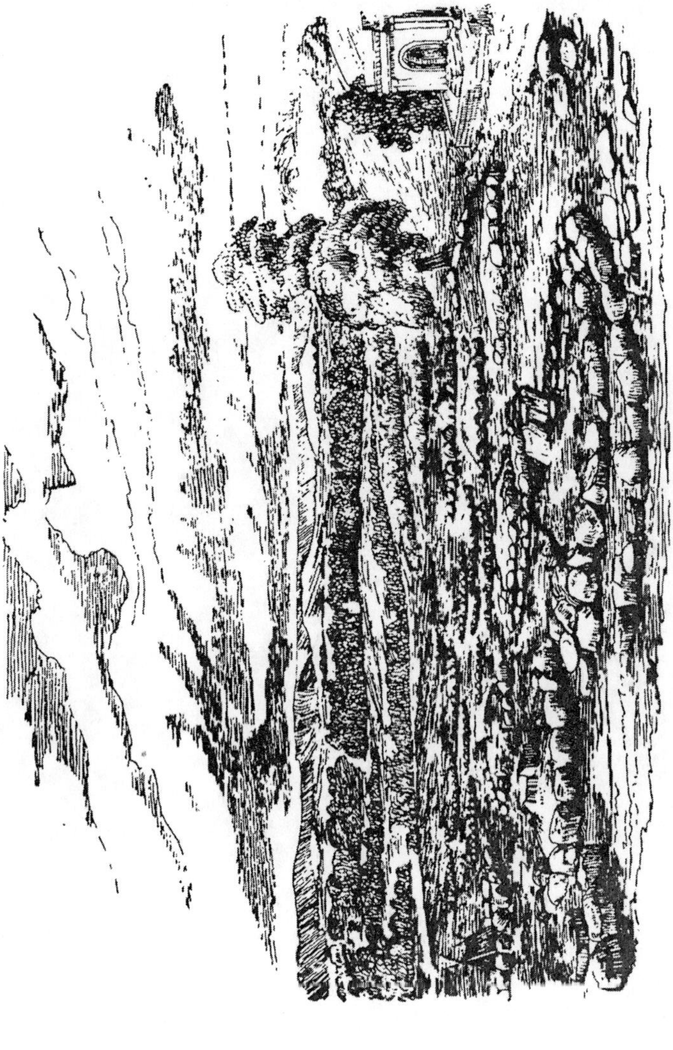

SKETCH NO. III
Cairn Cemetery, Jiwarji.

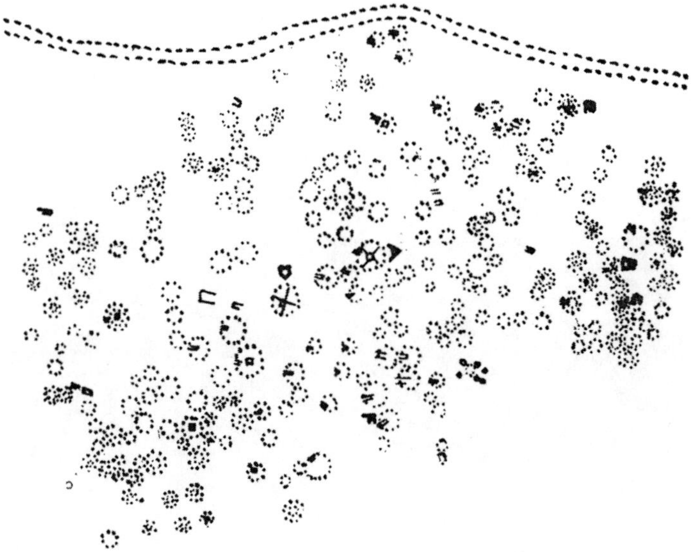

PLAN No. V

Plan of Cemetery of Cairns, Jiwarji, Shorapur. Scale 160 Feet=1 inch.

Section of Barrow over Cairn A, Jiwarji.

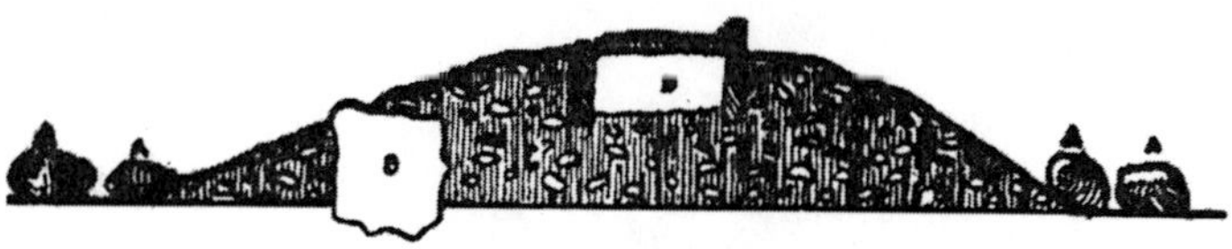

AA. Circle Stones.

B. Entrance Stones.

C. Tumulus of Earth and Stones.

C. Surface Cist.

CAIRN D.

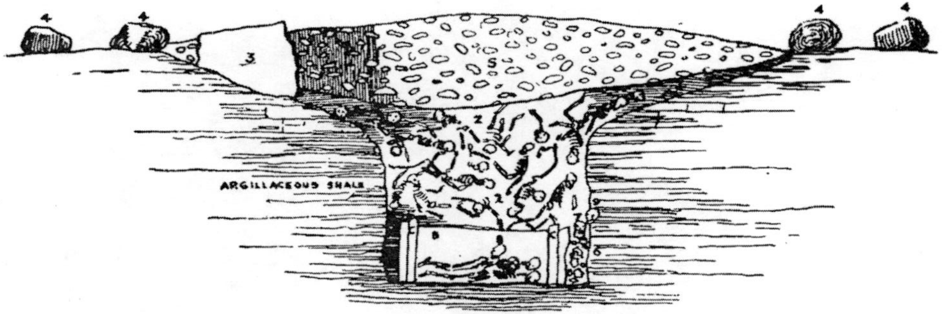

SECTION OF CAIRN D.

REFERENCES

1 LONGITUDINAL SECTION OF CIST, WITH TWO SKELETONS, FACES DOWNWARD
2.2.2 SPACE FILLED WITH GREY EARTH, AND SKELETONS IRREGULARLY THROWN IN.
3, ENTRANCE STONES, LIMESTONE SLABS, 2 FEET APART
4.4.4, OUTSIDE CIRCLE STONES.
5. LOOSE STONES AND EARTH.
6. SPACE FILLED WITH SMALL URNS.
7. SINGLE SKULL ON TOP OF URNS.
8. SINGLE SKULL ON TOP OF SKELETONS.
9. SINGLE SKULL ON LEDGE OF SHALE OVER URNS.

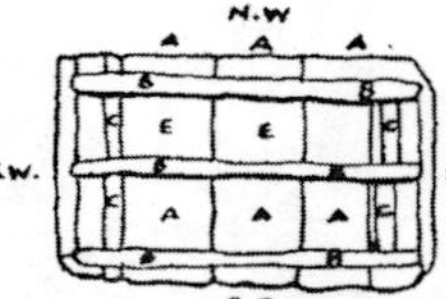

CAIRN D. GROUND PLAN OF CIST.

AA, SLABS OF LIMESTONE FOR FLOOR.
BB, UPRIGHT SLABS FOR SIDES.
CC, HEAD AND FOOT SLABS.
DD, TWO SKELETONS.
EE, PLACE FILLED IN WITH URNS.

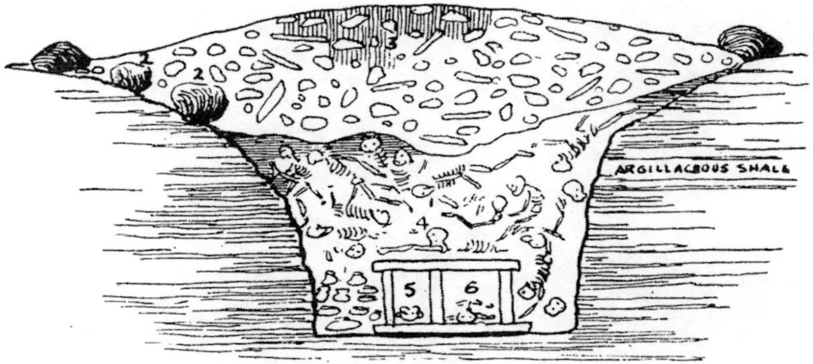

Section of Cairn E, *Jiwarji*, Fig. 1.

REFERENCES.

1 1, CIRCLE STONES.
2 2, STONES LEADING TO CIST.
3, STONES, SHALE, AND EARTH
4 4, SPACE FILLED WITH GREY EARTH AND CONFUSED SKELETONS
5, INTERIOR OF CIST; ONE SKELETON COMPLETE.
6, INTERIOR OF CIST, TWO SKELETONS, WITH ONE SKULL.
7, JARS AND URNS, WHOLE AND BROKEN.

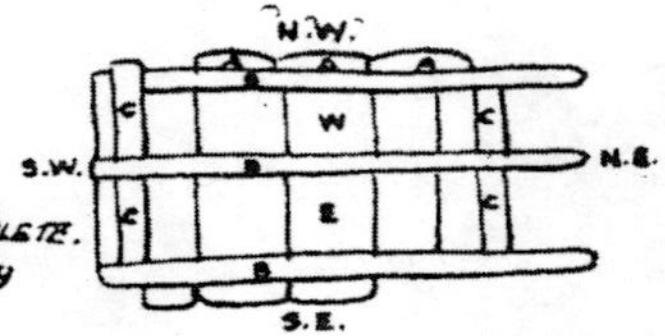

AA, FLOOR SLABS.
BB, UPRIGHT DO.
CC, HEAD AND FOOT PIECES.

PLATE XII

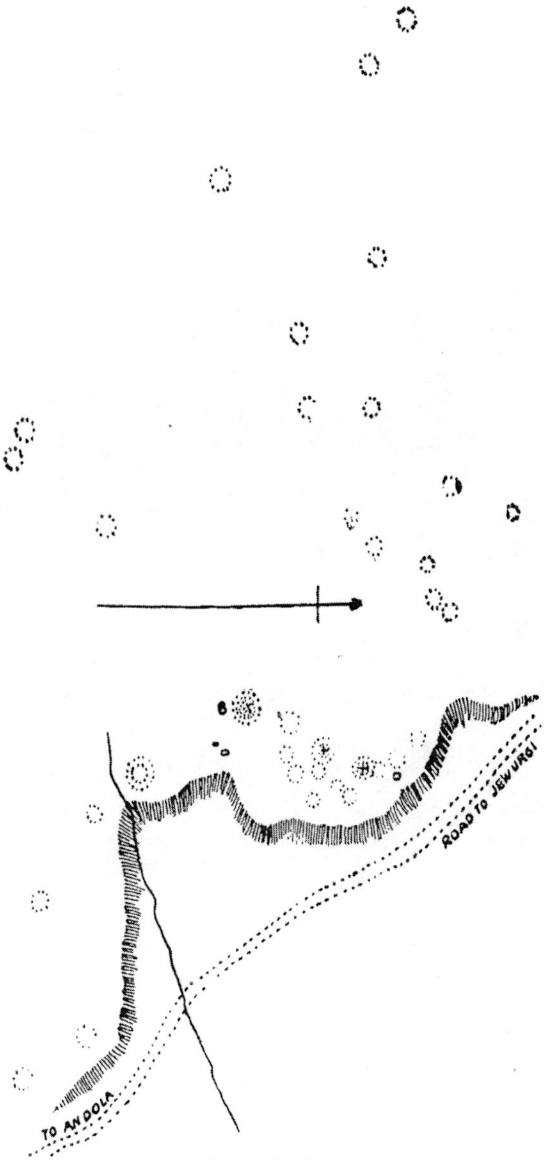

PLAN No. 6.

Cairns at Andola, Shorapoor.

PLATE XIII

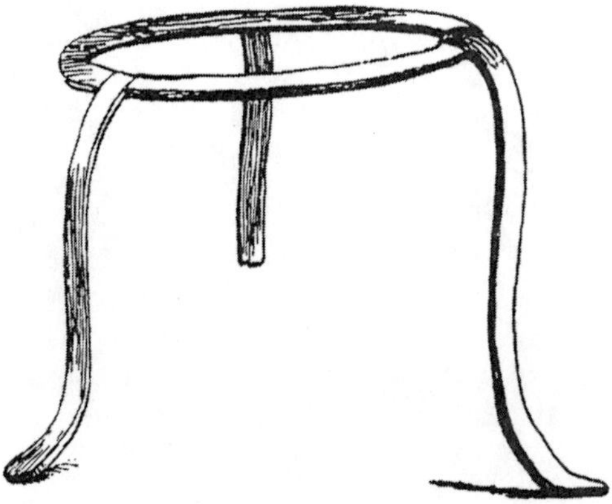

Iron Tripod, Cairn A, Andola, $\frac{1}{2}$ size.

Earthen Vessels, Andola Cairns, $\frac{1}{4}$ size.

Earthen Vessels, Jiwarji Cairns, $\frac{1}{6}$ size.

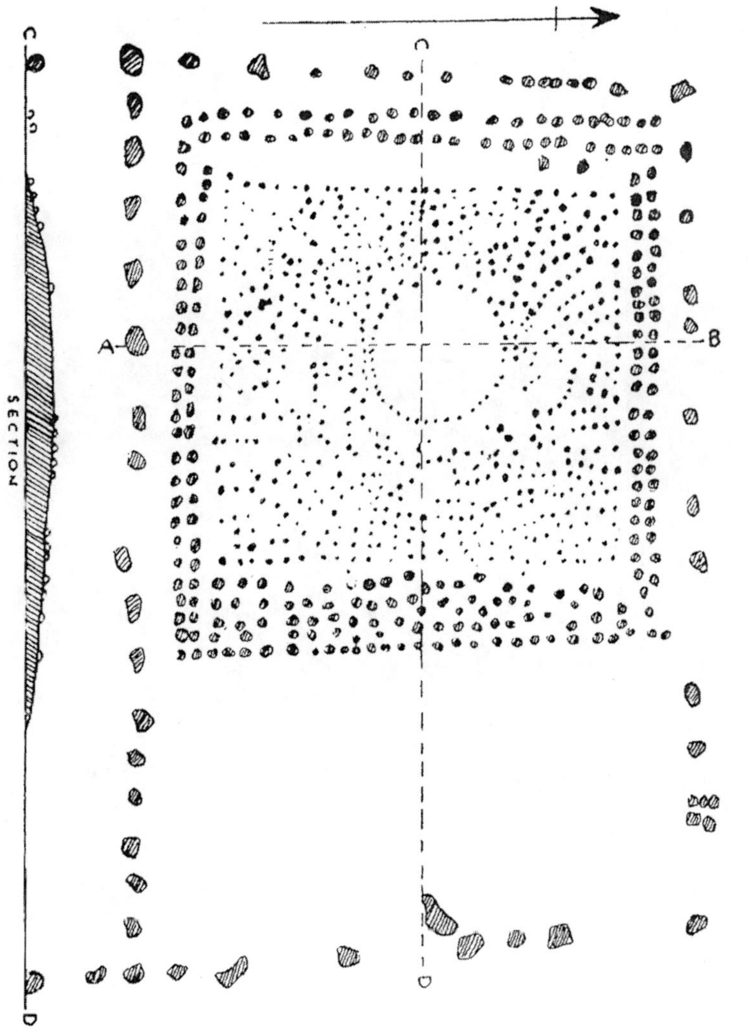

PLAN NO. 8

Shanpoor Tumulus. Scale 80 feet=1 inch.

SKETCH No. 12

East side of the Shahpoor Tumulus, showing the Granite Boundary Rocks and some of the Greenstone Boulders.

SKETCH No. 13

South side of Shahpoor Tumulus Boundary, Granite Kolas.

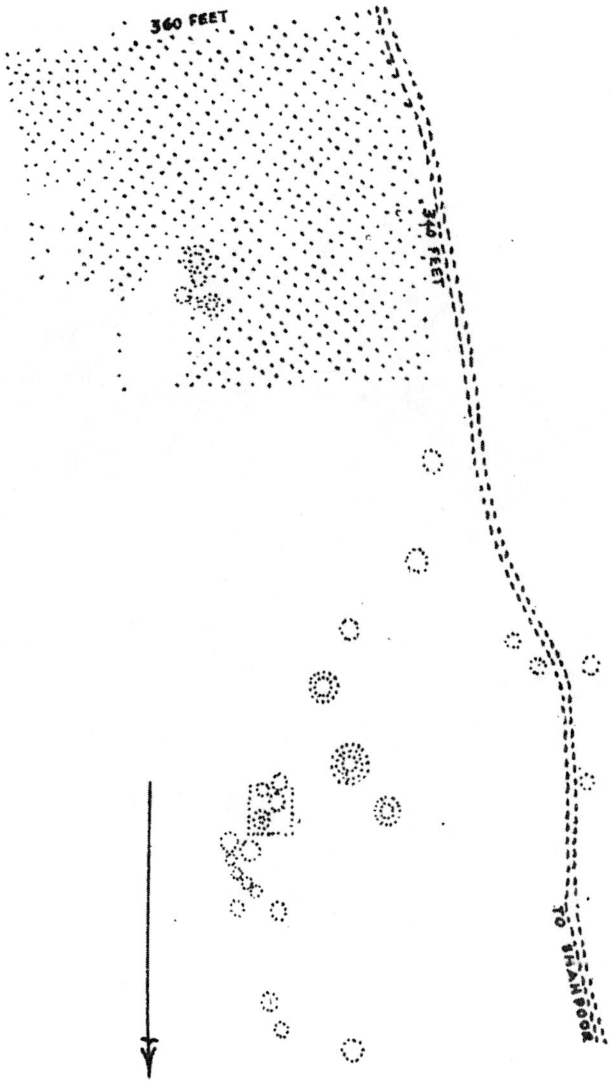

PLAN NO. 9

Cairn Cemetery at Vibathulli, near Shahpoor. Scale 160 feet = 1 inch.

PLATE XVII

PLAN NO. 10

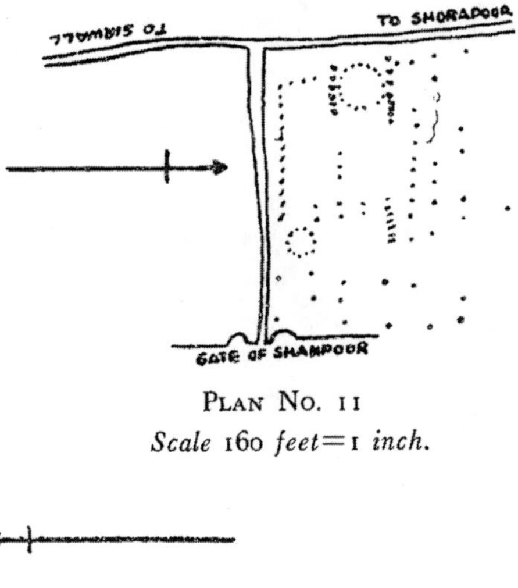

PLAN NO. 11
Scale 160 *feet*=1 *inch*.

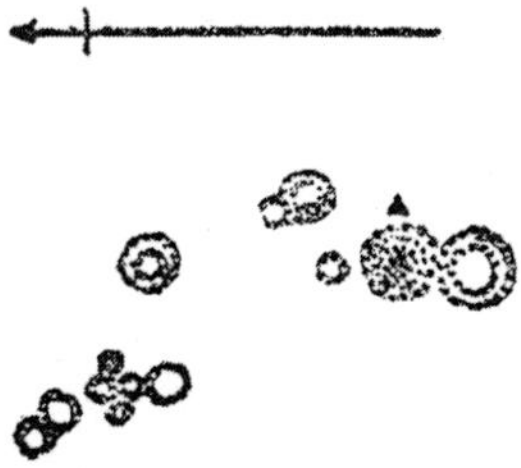

PLAN NO. 12.

PLATE XVIII

FIG. I HYDERABAD CAIRNS CAST BRONZE BELL, ½ SIZE

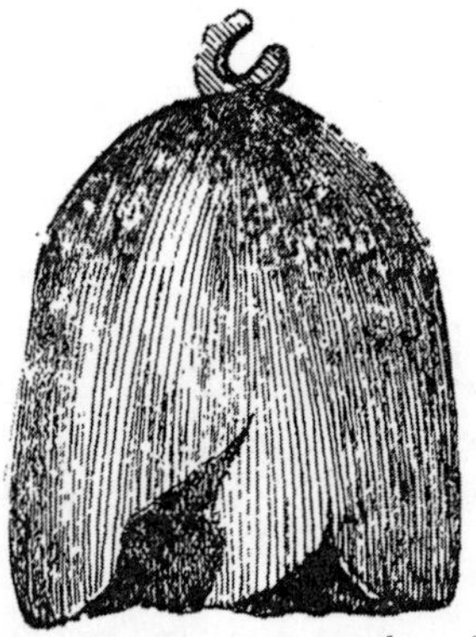

FIG II. HYDERABAD CAIRNS. WROUGHT COPPER BELL. ½ SIZE

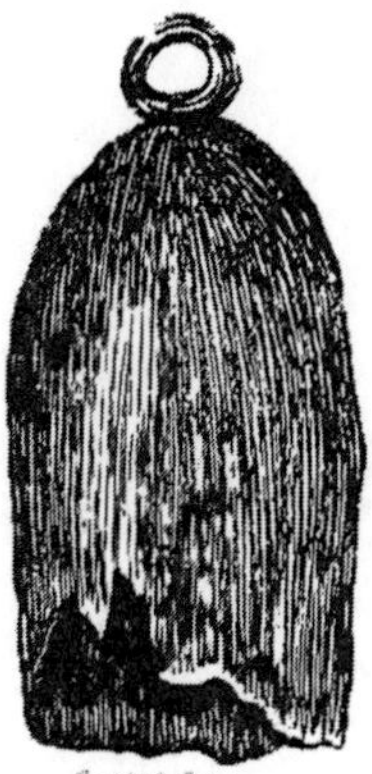

COPPER BELL ½ SIZE

ARROW HEADS, ½ SIZE

KNIFE, OR SICKLE ½ SIZE

Fig. III.